California
Preschool Learning Foundations

Volume 2

Visual and Performing Arts
Physical Development
Health

Publishing Information

The *California Preschool Learning Foundations* (Volume 2) was developed by the Child Development Division, California Department of Education. This publication was edited by Faye Ong, working in cooperation with Laura Bridges and Desiree Soto, Consultants, Child Development Division. It was designed and prepared for printing by the staff of CDE Press, with the cover and interior design created by Cheryl McDonald. It was published by the Department of Education, 1430 N Street, Sacramento, CA 95814-5901. It was distributed under the provisions of the Library Distribution Act and *Government Code* Section 11096.

©2010 by the California Department of Education
All rights reserved

ISBN 978-8011-1708-4

Ordering Information

Copies of this publication are available for sale from the California Department of Education. For prices and ordering information, please visit the Department Web site at http://www.cde.ca.gov/re/pn or call the CDE Press Sales Office at 1-800-995-4099. An illustrated *Educational Resource Catalog* describing publications, videos, and other instructional media available from the Department can be obtained without charge by writing to the CDE Press Sales Office, California Department of Education, 1430 N Street, Suite 3207, Sacramento, CA 95814-5901; faxing to 916-323-0823; or calling the CDE Press Sales Office at the telephone number shown above.

Notice

The guidance in the *California Preschool Learning Foundations* (Volume 2) is not binding on local educational agencies or other entities. Except for the statutes, regulations, and court decisions that are referenced herein, the documents is exemplary, and compliance with it is not mandatory. (See *Education Code* Section 33308.5.)

Contents

A Message from the State Superintendent
of Public Instruction
v

Acknowledgments
vii

Introduction
xi

**Foundations in the
Visual and Performing Arts**
1

**Foundations in
Physical Development**

**Foundations in
Health**

Appendix: The Foundations

A Message from the State Superintendent of Public Instruction

I am delighted to present the *California Preschool Learning Foundations (Volume 2)*. This publication is the second of a three-volume series designed to improve early learning and development for California's preschool children.

Young children are naturally eager to learn. However, not all of them enter kindergarten ready for school. All too often, children are already lagging behind their classmates, and this circumstance can impede their continued learning and development long past kindergarten. High-quality preschool teaching contributes to children's long-range social and academic success, as well as their ability to express themselves creatively through the arts, their capacity to engage in physically challenging activities, and their development of lifelong health habits.

Children who attend high-quality preschools benefit from rich opportunities to learn through play. They also benefit from curriculum that integrates all the developmental domains in a way that is developmentally, culturally, and linguistically appropriate.

Intentionally engaging children in play supports the learning and development that is described in the preschool learning foundations. In a recent report, the National Association for the Education of Young Children (NAEYC) calls for early educators to make play a regular part of the daily curriculum and be responsive to the needs of each student.

In addition, a recent report from the American Academy of Pediatrics concludes that play is vitally important for healthy brain development. These reports, as well as many others, make clear that preschool children's play and integrated learning are vital components of high-quality preschool programs.

With the goal of ensuring that all preschools in California offer high-quality programs, the California Department of Education collaborated with leading early childhood educators, researchers, advocates, and parents to develop Volume 2 of the preschool learning foundations.

The foundations outline key knowledge and skills that most children can achieve when provided with the kinds of interactions, instruction, and environments shown by research to promote early learning and development. Volume 2 focuses on three domains: visual and performing arts, physical development, and health. These domains often receive less attention than some of the other domains, but they are equally important for preschool children's overall learning and development.

As research that is summarized in this volume indicates, physical exercise and healthy routines and nutritional choices set the stage for lifelong healthy habits.

The recent NAEYC report underscores the need for children to play outside, use their large muscles, and engage in vigorous physical activities every day. Of course, the visual and performing arts fuel both preschool children's imaginative play and creativity and also promote learning in all domains, including physical skill development, cognitive development, and social-emotional development.

I believe that these foundations will help guide and support all California preschools in providing developmentally appropriate instruction and activities that engage young minds, hearts, and bodies. Such learning will lead to children's well-being and success throughout life.

JACK O'CONNELL
State Superintendent of Public Instruction

Acknowledgments

The development of Volume 2 of the *California Preschool Learning Foundations* involved many people. The following groups contributed: (1) project leaders; (2) lead researchers; (3) the expanded research consortia; (4) the preschool learning foundations research consortium; (5) staff from the California Department of Education; (6) early childhood education stakeholder organizations; (7) facilitators of the public input sessions and the participants; (8) participants in the Web posting process; and (9) participants in the public hearing process.

Project Leaders

The following staff members of WestEd are gratefully acknowledged for their contributions: **Peter Mangione, Charlotte Tilson,** and **Cathy Tsao.**

Lead Researchers

Special thanks are extended to the lead researchers for their expertise and contributions as lead writers.

Visual and Performing Arts

James Catterall, University of California, Los Angeles

Physical Development

Abbey Alkon, University of California, San Francisco

Victoria Leonard, University of California, San Francisco

Health

Abbey Alkon, University of California, San Francisco

Victoria Leonard, University of California, San Francisco

Expanded Research Consortia

The development of Volume 2 was guided by an expanded research consortium of experts in each domain. Domain experts and their affiliations are listed as follows. Thanks are extended to these individuals for contributing their expertise to this project and for collaborating with the preschool learning foundations research consortium.

Visual and Performing Arts

Liane Brouillette, University of California, Irvine

Victoria Brown, Lucy School

Lisa Catterall, Imagination Group

Joyce Jordan, University of Miami

Gwen Morgan-Beazell, Santa Ana College

Linda Neely, University of Connecticut

Nancy Ng, Luna Kids Dance

Physical Development

David Gallahue, Indiana University

Clersida Garcia, Northern Illinois University

Patricia Kimbrell, San Diego State University

Rebecca Lytle, California State University, Chico

Robyn Wu, Samuel Merritt University

Laura Vidal-Prudholme, Saddleback College

Health

Abbey Alkon, University of California, San Francisco

Jyu-Lin Chen, University of California, San Francisco

Charlotte Hendricks, Healthy Childcare Consultants, Inc.

Victoria Leonard, University of California, San Francisco

Sondra Moe, Rio Hondo College
Ken Springer, Southern Methodist University
Barbara Tinsley, Arizona State University

Preschool Learning Foundations Research Consortium

The following research consortium members are recognized for their knowledge and expertise in guiding the development process and for their expert review of the document to be reflective of California's young learners.

Cindy Bernheimer, WestEd
Melinda Brookshire, WestEd
Caroline Pietrangelo Owens, WestEd
Peter Mangione, WestEd
Katie Monahan, WestEd
Stephen Moore, University of California, Berkeley
Teresa Ragsdale, WestEd
Amy Schustz-Alvarez, WestEd
Charlotte Tilson, WestEd
Cathy Tsao, WestEd
Mark Wilson, University of California, Berkeley
Osnat Zur, WestEd

Advisers on English Language Development and Cultural Diversity

Alison Wishard Guerra, University of California, San Diego
Gisela Jia, The City University of New York
Rebeca Valdivia, WestEd
Ann-Marie Wiese, WestEd
Marlene Zepeda, California State University, Los Angeles

Universal Design Advisers

Maurine Ballard-Rosa, California State University, Sacramento
Meryl Berk, Vision Consultant, Early Education Programs & Services, San Diego County Office of Education
Linda Brault, WestEd

California Department of Education

Thanks are also extended to the following staff members: **Gavin Payne,** Chief Deputy Superintendent; **Anthony Monreal,*** Deputy Superintendent, Curriculum and Instruction Branch; **Camille Maben,** Director, Child Development Division; **Cecelia Fisher-Dahms,** Administrator, Quality Improvement Office; **Desiree Soto,** Consultant, and **Laura Bridges,** Consultant, Child Development Division; for ongoing revisions and recommendations. During the lengthy development process, many CDE staff members were involved at various levels. Additional thanks are extended to members of the Child Development Division: **Michael Jett,*** **Gwen Stephens,*** **Gail Brodie, Sy Dang Nguyen, Mary Smithberger,*** **Maria Trejo,** and **Charles Vail;** Special Education Division: **Meredith Cathcart;** Nutrition Services Division: **Lynette Haynes-Brown, Kelley Knapp,** and **Heather Reed;** Professional Development and Curriculum Support Division: **Nancy Carr.**

Early Childhood Education Stakeholder Organizations

Representatives from many statewide organizations provided perspectives affecting various aspects of the learning foundations.

Action Alliance for Children
Alliance for a Better Community
Asian Pacific Islander Community Action Network
Association of California School Administrators
Baccalaureate Pathways in Early Childhood Education (BPECE)

---

*During the development of the foundations, these individuals worked for the California Department of Education.

California Alliance Concerned with School-Age Parenting and Pregnancy Prevention (CACSAP/Cal-SAFE)
California Association for Bilingual Education (CABE)
California Association for the Education of Young Children (CAEYC)
California Association of Family Child Care (CAFCC)
California Association of Latino Superintendents and Administrators (CALSA)
California Child Care Coordinators Association
California Child Care Resource and Referral Network (CCCRRN)
California Child Development Administrators Association (CCDAA)
California Child Development Corps
California Commission for Teacher Credentialing
California Community College Early Childhood Educators (CCCECE)
California Community Colleges Chancellor's Office (CCCCO)
California County Superintendents Educational Services Association (CCSESA)
California Early Reading First Network
California Federation of Teachers (CFT)
California Head Start Association (CHSA)
California Kindergarten Association
California National Even Start Association
California Preschool Instructional Network
California Professors of Early Childhood Special Education (CAPECSE)
California School Boards Association
California State Parent-Teacher Association
California State University Office of the Chancellor
California Teachers Association
California Tomorrow
Californians Together
Campaign for High Quality Early Learning Standards in California
Child Development Policy Institute
Children Now
The Children's Collabrium
Council for Exceptional Children/The California Division for Early Childhood (Cal DEC)
Council of CSU Campus Childcare (CCSUCC)
Curriculum Alignment Project
Curriculum & Instruction Steering Committee
English Language Learners Preschool Coalition (ELLPC)
Fight Crime, Invest in Kids California
First 5 Association of California
First 5 California Children & Families Commission
Infant Development Association of California (IDA)
Learning Disabilities Association of California
Los Angeles Universal Preschool (LAUP)
Mexican American Legal Defense and Education Fund (MALDEF)
Migrant Education Even Start (MEES)
Migrant Head Start
National Black Child Development Institute (NBCDI)
National Council of La Raza (NCLR)
Packard Foundation Children, Families, and Communities Program
Preschool California
Professional Association for Childhood Education (PACE)
Special Education Local Plan Area (SELPA) Organization
University of California Child Care Directors
University of California Office of the President (UCOP)
Voices for African-American Students, Inc. (VAAS)
Zero to Three

Public Input Sessions

Special thanks are also extended to **Nancy Herota, Natalie Woods Andrews,** and the California Preschool Instructional Network regional leads; and **Melinda Brookshire, Jenna Bilmes,** and **Jan Davis,** WestEd, for their contributions in facilitating 54 public input sessions on the draft foundations. Thanks also to the participants in the public input sessions for their contributions to this project.

Introduction

The preschool learning foundations are a critical step in the California Department of Education's (CDE's) efforts to strengthen preschool education and close the school-readiness gap in California, thereby narrowing the achievement gap during the K–12 school years. The foundations describe competencies—knowledge and skills—that most children can be expected to exhibit in a high-quality program as they complete their first or second year of preschool. In other words, the foundations are destination points of learning that, with appropriate support, children move toward and often reach during the preschool years.

The foundations are designed to promote understanding of young children's development of knowledge and skills and to help with considering appropriate ways to support children's learning. In essence, the foundations serve as a cornerstone for educating practitioners about children's learning and development. The foundations are designed to be used in combination with other sources of information: formal educational course work on early learning and development, information on individual differences, including those related to disabilities, knowledge about the contribution of cultural and linguistic experiences to early development, and English-language development, including the CDE's resource guide *Preschool English Learners: Principles and Practices to Promote Language, Literacy, and Learning* (2009), insights from children's families, and the practical experiences of preschool teachers and program directors.

The support needed to attain the competencies varies from child to child. Many children learn simply by participating in high-quality preschool programs. Such programs offer children environments and experiences that encourage active playful exploration and experimentation. With play as an integral part of the curriculum, high-quality programs include purposeful teaching to help children gain knowledge and skills.

With regard to the visual and performing arts, physical development, and health foundations in this volume, children can demonstrate their knowledge and skills using any language or, for most of the foundations, through nonverbal means. Many children effectively apply their often more-advanced ability in their home language to understand, for example, art, music, drama, and dance concepts; movement concepts; and health concepts. Other children may have a disability or special need that requires particular adaptations.[1] To serve all children, preschool programs must work to provide appropriate conditions for learning and assist each child to move along a pathway of learning and healthy development.

All 50 states have either developed preschool standards or are in the process of doing so. Many states have aligned early learning standards with their kindergarten content standards. In most cases, those alignment efforts have focused on academic content areas, such as English–language arts or mathematics. In California, priority has been placed on aligning expectations for preschool learning with the state's kindergarten academic content standards and on complementing those content areas with attention to social-emotional development and English-language development. Like the learning in such domains as language and literacy and mathematics, the concepts in social-emotional development and English-language development also contribute significantly to young children's readiness for school (*From Neurons to Neighborhoods* 2000; *Eager to Learn* 2000; *Early Learning Standards* 2002). Because the focus on preschool learning in California includes the full range of developmental domains, the term *foundations* is used rather than *standards*. This term is intended to convey that learning in every domain affects young children's readiness for school.

Content of This Volume

The preschool learning foundations presented in this volume cover the following domains:

- Visual and Performing Arts
- Physical Development
- Health

Those domains represent crucial areas of learning and development for young children. The foundations within a particular domain provide a thorough overview of development in that domain. Preschool children's knowledge and skills can be considered from the perspective of one domain, such as physical development or visual and performing arts. Yet when taking an in-depth look at one domain, one needs to keep in mind that learning is an integrated experience for young children. For example, a young child may concentrate on a performing art, such as dance, but the experience also pertains to learning in the cognitive, social, linguistic, physical, and health domains. The relationships between learning domains are particularly apparent with physical development and visual and performing arts. Indeed, many of the same movement concepts and skills appear in the foundations of both domains.

The foundations written for each of the domains are based on research and evidence and are enhanced with expert practitioners' suggestions and examples. The purpose of the foundations is to promote understanding of preschool children's learning and to guide instructional practice. It is anticipated that teachers, administrators, parents, and policymakers will use the foundations as a springboard to prepare all young children for success in school.

Visual and Performing Arts Domain

The foundations for visual and performing arts address a wide range of competencies that preschool children

---

[1] Adaptations should be coordinated with the child's family and any specialist working with the child.

will need support to learn. The foundations focus on the following four strands:

- *Visual Art*, which includes noticing, responding to, and engaging in visual art; developing skills; and creating, inventing, and expressing through visual art
- *Music*, which covers noticing, responding to, and engaging in music; developing skills; and creating, inventing, and expressing through music
- *Drama*, which focuses on noticing, responding to, and engaging in drama; and developing skills to create, invent, and express through drama
- *Dance*, which centers on noticing, responding to, and engaging in dance; developing skills; and creating, inventing, and expressing through dance

The foundations written for this domain reflect the many ways in which young children experience the joys of learning, creativity, self-expression, and playful exploration. The arts provide varied and meaningful opportunities for children to engage in integrated learning experiences that contribute to their development in all domains.

Physical Development Domain

The physical development domain consists of the following three strands:

- *Fundamental Movement Skills*, which include balance, locomotor skills, and manipulative skills
- *Perceptual–Motor Skills and Movement Concepts*, which focus on body awareness, spatial awareness, and directional awareness
- *Active Physical Play*, which addresses active participation, cardiovascular endurance, muscular strength, muscular endurance, and flexibility

The competencies covered by the physical development domain center on what preschool children do much of the day. This area of development describes many avenues for young children's play, engagement with others, exploration, and learning.

Health Domain

Young children's development of health knowledge, attitudes, habits, and behaviors is receiving increasing attention in research and practice. The health foundations are divided into the following three strands:

- *Health Habits*, which cover basic hygiene, oral health, knowledge of wellness, and sun safety
- *Safety*, which focuses on injury prevention
- *Nutrition*, which addresses nutrition knowledge, nutrition choices, and the self-regulation of eating

Preschool programs can promote young children's learning in this domain by giving young children opportunities to observe and participate in health-related practices and interactions. Children learn health-related routines and habits when caring adults convey the importance of those routines through modeling and encouragement.

Organization of the Foundations

Each strand of a domain consists of substrands, and the foundations are organized under the substrands. Foundations are presented for children at around 48 months of age and at around 60 months of age. In some cases the difference between the foundations at 48 months and 60 months is more pronounced than for the other foundations. Even so, the foundations focus on 48 and 60 months of age because they correspond to the end of the first and second years of preschool. In all cases, the foundation at around 60 months of age builds on the corresponding foundation at around 48 months of age. In other words, for each foundation the age levels are two points on a continuum of learning. Of course, teachers need to know where each child is on a continuum of learning throughout the child's time in preschool.

The Desired Results Developmental Profile, Preschool (DRDP PS), which is currently being aligned to the foundations, gives teachers a means to observe children's learning along a continuum of four developmental levels (Exploring, Developing, Building, and Integrating). On the continuum, children at the Exploring level start to become familiar with a new knowledge area and, in a basic way, try out skills they are starting to learn. At the next level, Developing, children begin to demonstrate basic mastery in a knowledge and skill area. At the Building level, children refine and expand their knowledge and skills in an area of learning. At the Integrating level, they connect the knowledge and skills they have mastered in one area with those in other areas. The Desired Results Developmental Profile *access* provides a means to observe the knowledge and skills of preschool children with disabilities whose development is best described within a range from birth to five years.

The examples listed under each foundation suggest a range of possible ways in which children can demonstrate the competency addressed by a foundation. The examples illustrate the different contexts in which children may show the competencies reflected in the foundations. Examples highlight that children learn while they engage in imaginative play, explore the environment and materials, make discoveries, are inventive, or interact with peers, teachers, or other adults. Many examples include children using language to express themselves. Nevertheless, children can demonstrate learning in these domains in any language. For instance, children who are English learners will often be creative, inventive, or expressive through drama and singing in their home language. Although often illustrative of the diversity of young children's learning experiences, the examples listed under a foundation are not exhaustive. In fact, teachers often observe other ways in which young children demonstrate the competency addressed by a foundation.

The Appendix, "The Foundations," contains a summary list of the foundations in each domain without examples.

Universal Design for Learning

The California preschool learning foundations are guides to support preschool programs in their efforts to foster the learning and development of all young children in California, including children who have disabilities. It is important to provide opportunities to follow different pathways to learning in the preschool foundations in order to make them helpful for all of California's children. To that end, the California preschool learning foundations incorporate a concept known as *universal design* for learning.

The Center for Applied Special Technology (CAST) developed the principles of universal design for learning based on the understanding that children learn in different ways (CAST 2007). In today's diverse preschool settings and programs, the use of a curriculum accessible to all learners is critical to successful early learning. Universal design for learning is not a single approach that will accommodate everyone; rather, it refers to providing multiple approaches to learning in order to meet the needs of diverse learners. Universal design provides for multiple means of representation, multiple means of engagement, and multiple means of expression (CAST 2007). *Multiple means of representation* refers to providing information in a variety of ways so the learning needs of all of the children are met. *Multiple means of expression* refers to allowing children to use alternative methods to demonstrate what they know or what they are feeling. *Multiple means of engagement* refers to providing choices for activities in the setting or program that facilitate learning by building on children's interests.

The examples given in the preschool learning foundations have been worded to depict the many ways in which children receive information and express themselves.

- When consistent with the content being illustrated, the terms *communicates* and *responds* are used in examples rather than "says." "Communicates" and "responds" are inclusive of any language and any form of communication, including speaking, sign language, pictures, electronic communication devices, eye-pointing, gesturing, and so forth.
- The terms "identifies" and "indicates" or "points to" are used to represent multiple means of indicating objects, people, or events in the environment. Examples include the use of gestures, eye-pointing, nodding, or responding *yes* or *no* when another person points to or touches an object.

When reading each foundation and the accompanying examples, teachers can consider the means by which a child with a disability might best acquire information and demonstrate competence in those areas. It is essential to include a child's special education teacher, parents, or related service provider when environments, curriculum, and adaptations are being planned. In addressing the individual needs of children, early childhood educators need to consider the enormous variation in children's growth and development across all developmental domains.

For example, a child with physical disabilities and visual impairments may understand many of the movement concepts without being able to demonstrate them in the same way as other children. Although the child may show delays in one area of development, this tendency does not necessarily indicate delays in cognitive development as well as other areas of development. The distinction is important to keep in mind because if an early childhood educator expects a child who cannot see or physically move to demonstrate a level of understanding, the child's cognitive abilities may be underestimated because the child cannot consistently and broadly show the expected level. Even with the appropriate specialized instruction, materials, and adaptations, the child may still show cognitive delays. The preschool years are a time of critical cognitive growth and concept development, and one cannot assume that this development will still occur in children with disabilities when a sensory or motor disability is present. It is essential that teachers collaborate with family members and special educators to ensure that all children having disabilities are provided with effective preschool experiences and appropriate educational services and supports.

The Foundations and Preschool Learning in California

The foundations are at the heart of the CDE's approach to promoting preschool learning. Teachers use best practices, curricular strategies, and instructional techniques that assist children in learning the knowledge and skills described in the preschool learning foundations. The "how-tos" of teaching young children include setting up environments, supporting children's self-initiated play, selecting appropriate materials, and planning and implementing teacher-guided learning activities.

Two major considerations underlie the "how-tos" of teaching. First, teachers can effectively foster early learning by thoughtfully considering the preschool learning foundations as they plan environments and activities. And second, during every step in the planning for young children's learning, teachers have an opportunity to tap into the prominent role of play. Teachers can best support young children by both encouraging the rich learning that occurs in children's self-initiated play and by introducing purposeful instructional activities that playfully engage preschoolers in learning.

Professional development is a key component of early care and education in fostering preschool learning. The foundations can become a unifying element for both preservice and in-service professional development. Preschool program directors and teachers can use the foundations to facilitate curriculum planning and implementation. At the center of the CDE's evolving system for supporting young children during the preschool years, the foundations are designed to help teachers be intentional and focus their efforts on the knowledge and skills that all young children need to acquire for success in preschool and early elementary school—and throughout life.

References

Center for Applied Special Technology. 2007. Universal design for learning. http://www.cast.org/udl/ (accessed June 8, 2007).

Eager to Learn: Educating Our Preschoolers. 2000. Edited by B. T. Bowman, M. S. Donovan, and M. S. Burns. Washington, DC: National Academy Press.

Early Learning Standards: Creating the Conditions for Success. 2002. Washington, DC: National Association for the Education of Young Children.

From Neurons to Neighborhoods: The Science of Early Childhood Development. 2000. Edited by J. P. Shonkoff and D. A. Phillips. Washington, DC: National Academy Press.

Preschool English Learners: Principles and Practices to Promote Language, Literacy, and Learning (Second edition). 2009. Sacramento: California Department of Education.

Scott-Little, C; S. L. Kagan; and V. S. Firelow. 2006. Conceptualization of readiness and the content of early learning standards: The intersection of policy and research. *Early Childhood Research Quarterly* 21: 153–73.

FOUNDATIONS IN THE
Visual and Performing Arts

The visual and performing arts offer preschool children many ways to experience playful exploration, self-expression, creativity, and the joy of learning. The arts also support preschool children's learning and development in varied and meaningful ways. Preschool children are interested in visual art, music, drama, and dance. Teachers have many opportunities to observe children's enthusiasm for creating art. They provide experiences that promote artistic expression through their teaching practices. During the preschool period, the arts are more about the *process* (in the sense of participation, engagement, and involvement) than about the *product*, or the end result, of artistic activity. All children can participate in and enjoy the arts, including children with disabilities and other special needs. The arts are important in the world of preschoolers, as children have the chance to use their imaginations while learning. Through the arts, children draw upon their interests, experiences, and personalities as they express themselves, create with others, and participate in their preschool community.

The visual and performing arts provide a means for children to grow in understanding themselves and the world around them. Children receive opportunities to draw inspiration from the environment and their experiences to create and to communicate through art, individually and with others. Art engages English learners and children whose home culture might be different from the preschool culture. Participation in the arts helps children develop language skills. The social context of arts activities supports English learners, who can participate as their language skills develop. Participation in visual arts, music, drama, and dance offers a way for children to join in social interactions with other children and adults. It provides both physical and social prompts to advance shared meaning with others.

Art can also serve as a meaningful way to create a strong sense of community in the classroom. The arts provide opportunities for children to participate in the shared cultural practices of the program. Through the arts, a preschool environment can be created that includes and celebrates children from diverse linguistic and cultural backgrounds. The arts provide opportunities for children to express themselves, demonstrate competence,

and show creativity in ways that may not depend on language. For children from diverse linguistic or cultural communities, arts-based activities can provide a link between home and preschool. Teachers welcome children's cultures to preschool programs when they encourage children and families to share songs, dances, poems, music, visual art, or art-related objects and practices from home. Programs serving diverse children can create positive learning opportunities, culturally relevant curricula, and a sense of community by including visual and performing arts that represent the children's home cultures.

Art, Artistic Play, and Learning

Preschool children enthusiastically take part in the arts. Their attraction to and interest in the arts can provide valuable information about their learning and development. Preschool children take part in artistic activity frequently and with great interest. Through their engagement in art, preschool children grow in their understanding of their world, the ability to problem-solve, and the ability to represent ideas. Familiarity with art materials supports children's creativity. Children with disabilities can also participate in the arts with enthusiasm and interest, with the use of adapted materials or tools as needed.

Preschool children's artistic efforts are often directed at producing physical or mental images through drawings, body movements, or pretend characters. This is called representation. The artistic representations of preschoolers tend toward the literal (for example, *This drawing is a fish,* or *I'm pretending I'm a lion).* Even younger preschoolers use forms of symbolism within their representations. For example, when asked to pick a song about a lazy summer day, the child may choose music with soft and slow qualities. Children try, consider, and refine the symbols they use in their art, thereby learning more about what they are trying to represent.

Of course, representation is not the exclusive domain of the visual and performing arts. Representing ideas and things is fundamental to human communication. Representation lies at the heart of spoken and written language. A crucial link between the arts and more general development is found here. Research suggests that learning and development in the arts provides an underpinning for literacy and language development, in part, through cultivating representation skills. The many interrelationships between the arts and other areas of child development further indicate the importance of the arts during the preschool years.

Play is crucial to all areas of children's learning and development, including social-emotional, language, and cognitive and physical development. Art at the preschool level involves play and exploration. Play provides children with opportunities to experiment and be creative, for example, through molding clay, dancing to music, or role-playing. Preschool children take part in the arts in playful ways, learning along the way.

Child Development in the Arts

Some skills, knowledge, and behavior emerge in nearly all children as a consequence of daily experience. Many arts-related developments (for example, the progression of drawing skills) tend to be seen at particular ages or in a particular sequence.

Although some behaviors and skills in the arts develop more or less naturally through the course of children's everyday experience, others need the support of adult guidance and intentional teaching: for example, using art implements, playing an instrument, dancing a sequence of steps, or shaping a body or facial expression to achieve dramatic effect. Teachers also help children acquire knowledge about the arts; for example, types of music or dance.

Organization of the Visual and Performing Arts Domain

The preschool foundations for the visual and performing arts describe the visual and performing arts knowledge, skills, and behaviors that preschool children typically develop in a quality preschool environment. The four strands in the visual and performing arts domain are Visual Art, Music, Drama, and Dance. Within each substrand, the foundations describe the knowledge and skills most children demonstrate at around 48 months of age and around 60 months of age. However, it is important to understand that the foundations are age-related and not age-dependent.

The foundations are illustrated by examples that put behavior in context. The examples show what the foundation might look like in a particular child. When examples are given that indicate verbal expression, the child may use any language or other form of communication (such as American Sign Language or picture exchange). For more information about children's second-language development please see *California Preschool Learning Foundations, Volume 1* (2008), in English Language Development.

Bibliographic notes are provided later. They offer further information and references to the research that informs this chapter.

The visual and performing arts domain comprises four strands. Each strand represents an arts discipline.

- Visual Art
- Music
- Drama
- Dance

Within the strands of Visual Art, Music, and Dance, there are three substrands:

- 1.0 Notice, Respond, and Engage
- 2.0 Develop Skills
- 3.0 Create, Invent, and Express

Within the Drama strand, there are two substrands:

- 1.0 Notice, Respond, and Engage
- 2.0 Develop Skills to Create, Invent, and Express Through Drama

Connections Through the Arts

Learning in one art form often connects to learning in the other art forms and developmental domains. Learning and development in the arts promotes learning and development in many other areas. The visual and performing arts foundations reflect the integrated nature of young children's learning.

- Children practice working together and learn about themselves and others as the arts often involve social interaction, social relationships, and social skills.
- Children build language as they make, respond to, and think about art.
- Children make connections between their own cultures and the cultures represented in the arts.

- Children benefit psychologically from the increasing competence they develop as they participate in the arts (for example, in painting, acting, dancing, or drumming).

Development of the Foundations

The development of the foundations in the visual and performing arts was a collaborative effort. It included a review of research, review of the *Visual and Performing Arts Content Standards for California Public Schools* (2001), review of state standards in the visual arts from other states, and review of input from practitioners, scholars, and stakeholder organizations.

The substrands are as follows:

Notice, Respond, and Engage. This substrand describes children's interest and enjoyment in the arts, for example, in drawing, making sculpture, singing to music, acting, or dancing. To *notice* is to orient attention to something. To *respond* is to interact with the materials and methods of an art form. This response may be subtle (for example, a glance, a smile, or stopping an activity). To *engage* is to sustain attention and interest over time.

Develop Skills. This substrand refers to the basic skills of performing, inventing, and creating through the arts. Examples of skills include the ability to draw a line or circle, to use a paintbrush, to follow the beat or tempo of a march, and to control arm and body movements in dance.

Create, Invent, and Express. This substrand describes how children use their skills to participate, express, invent, and create through the arts. Preschool children spend much of their time creating, inventing, and expressing themselves, and they use various means and approaches to do so.

Develop Skills to Create, Invent, and Express Through Drama. In contrast to visual art, music, and dance, skill development in drama overlaps with creative expression and hinges on early development of language, control of movement, and a conception of what it means to pretend. Therefore, in Drama the skill and expression substrands are consolidated into one.

Overview of the Foundations

Visual Art
1.0 Notice, Respond, and Engage
 1.1, 1.2, 1.3, 1.4
2.0 Develop Skills in Visual Art
 2.1, 2.2, 2.3, 2.4, 2.5, 2.6
3.0 Create, Invent, and Express Through Visual Art
 3.1, 3.2, 3.3

Music
1.0 Notice, Respond, and Engage
 1.1, 1.2, 1.3, 1.4
2.0 Develop Skills in Music
 2.1, 2.2
3.0 Create, Invent, and Express Through Music
 3.1, 3.2, 3.3

Drama
1.0 Notice, Respond, and Engage
 1.1, 1.2, 1.3
2.0 Develop Skills to Create, Invent, and Express Through Drama
 2.1, 2.2

Dance
1.0 Notice, Respond, and Engage
 1.1, 1.2, 1.3, 1.4
2.0 Develop Skills in Dance
 2.1, 2.2, 2.3
3.0 Create, Invent, and Express Through Dance
 3.1, 3.2, 3.3, 3.4

Visual Art

1.0 Notice, Respond, and Engage

At around 48 months of age	*At around 60 months of age*
1.1 Notice and communicate about objects or forms that appear in art.	**1.1** Communicate about elements appearing in art (such as line, texture, or perspective), and describe how objects are positioned in the artwork.
Examples	**Examples**
• Identifies a cow in a painting of a farm by verbalizing, pointing, or touching. • Points to a sculpture and communicates, "It's a horse." • Communicates, while looking at a painting of a tree, "That's like the tree in our yard. It's big and tall." • A visually impaired child comments, "I made this part bumpy and this part smooth" (running his hand across the paint).	• When shown a painting of a tree, describes shape of the tree and the sky in the background. • Looking at a painting, communicates, "There's a house, and there are flowers in front of the house. And there's a balloon far, far away." • A child who is visually impaired describes his art in sensory terms that relate to his experience: for example, "This _____ feels smooth." • When working on a collage, communicates, "I need more flowers for my picture."
1.2 Create marks with crayons, paints, and chalk and then identify them; mold and build with dough and clay and then identify them.	**1.2** Begin to plan art and show increasing care and persistence in completing it.
Examples	**Examples**
• Makes similar marks with a crayon over and over. • Hammers, flattens, and rolls clay or dough into a "worm" and shows it to another child. • During outdoor time, mounds wet sand to form a shape and says, "I'm making a castle."	• Communicates, "I'm going to draw Mommy" and then draws a person with hair and facial features. • In wet sand area, communicates, "Let's build a bridge" and then makes a mound with tunnels underneath. • Communicates, "I'm making pizza" and makes a clay pizza, adding bits of clay to represent favorite toppings.

1.0 Notice, Respond, and Engage (Continued)

At around 48 months of age	*At around 60 months of age*
1.3 Enjoy and engage with displays of visual art, inside or outside the classroom. Begin to express preferences for some art activities or materials.	**1.3** Enjoy and engage with displays of visual art. May expand critical assessment of visual art to include preferences for types of artwork or art activities.
Examples	**Examples**
• When looking at a painting of a landscape, communicates, "I want to go there." • Indicates which paintings she likes best when prompted. • Asks, "Can I finger paint? It's my favorite." • Waits in line for turn at the easel. • A child who is visually impaired expresses preference for textured art materials.	• When viewing a photo of a Navajo rug, communicates, "I like it because the colors are pretty, and it has zigzag lines all over." • Communicates, "I like when we make clay beads and paint them."
1.4 Choose own art for display in the classroom or for inclusion in a portfolio or book and briefly explain choice.	**1.4** Choose own art for display in the classroom or for inclusion in a portfolio or book and explain her or his ideas in some detail.
Examples	**Examples**
• Indicates one work when the teacher asks which of three paintings should go on the wall. When the teacher asks why that painting was chosen, responds, "Because I like it!" • Communicates, "This is my best one because it has sparkles." • After making clay object, says, "I'm going to give this to my mommy because it's pretty."	• Indicates one work when the teacher asks which of three paintings should go on the wall. When the teacher asks why that painting was chosen, responds, "This is the best one because it has my favorite colors." • Selects two clay bowls, one painted pink and the other red; communicates, "These should be on the shelf because they go together." • Selects a painting and communicates, "It's a picture of my family," then identifies mother, grandmother, and brother.

2.0 Develop Skills in Visual Art

At around 48 months of age	*At around 60 months of age*
2.1 Make straight and curved marks and lines; begin to draw rough circle shapes.	**2.1** Draw single circle and add lines to create representations of people and things.
Examples • Uses finger to draw lines on a window "fogged-up" with condensation. • Draws groups of vertical lines over and over on pieces of paper using a crayon. • Begins to draw circles over vertical and crossed lines (mandalas). • Draws a circle with two lines coming out of it and calls it a person.	**Examples** • Uses two circles, one for a body and one for a head, then adds arms and legs to create a "potato person." • Uses stick to draw circle and lines in the sand and calls it *la tortuga* (the turtle). • Draws separated curved lines using colored markers to represent a rainbow.
2.2 Begin to create paintings or drawings that suggest people, animals, and objects.	**2.2** Begin to create representative paintings or drawings that approximate or depict people, animals, and objects.
Examples • A child with a physical disability draws own family using a larger or adapted crayon. • Using a large paintbrush, first paints some areas green and then uses a smaller paintbrush to make orange dots scattered among the green areas. Says, "This is a pumpkin patch." • Draws what was seen at a Mardi Gras parade and shows the colorful drawings to the teacher. • Draws a roundish form on a fogged-up window and communicates, "That's my sister."	**Examples** • Draws a big banana, colors it green, brings it to the teacher, and says, "This is my *platano*."* • Paints the sun as a round yellow circle. • Uses finger paint and, on own initiative, adds a moon and a tree to the finished work. • Draws a dragon and asks the teacher, "Do we have gold crayons? I need to color the dragon."†

Note: Many examples in substrand 2.0 describe the child drawing or manipulating objects or developing motor control. Children with motor impairments may need assistance from an adult or peer to manipulate objects in order to do things such as draw, paint, sculpt, tear, or color. A child might also use adaptive materials (such as large manipulatives that are easy to grasp). Alternately, a child might demonstrate knowledge in these areas using assistive technology. For example, a child might use an electronic switch to start and stop a paintbrush on paper. Children with visual impairments might be offered materials for manipulating, painting, or gluing that are easily distinguishable by touch. Containers and trays of materials clearly define their work space and engage children who have visual impairments.

*Plantains are often a common part of children's diets in Latino and Caribbean countries.
†Ancient Chinese dragons are the ultimate symbols of cosmic *chi* (energy). The dragon is the most potent symbol of good fortune in the Chinese pantheon of symbols. As one of the four creatures of the world's directions, the dragon stands for new beginnings. Continued success, high achievement, and prosperity are also among the dragon's arsenal of good qualities, which contribute to its popularity.

2.0 Develop Skills in Visual Art *(Continued)*

At around 48 months of age	*At around 60 months of age*
2.3 Make somewhat regular-shaped balls and coils out of dough or clay.	**2.3** Make more representational forms out of dough or clay, using tools (for example, a rolling pin or a garlic press).
Examples	**Examples**
• Flattens out a piece of dough, and rolls it out while commenting, "I'm making *roti*."* • Makes dumplings from different colors of play dough, puts them on a plate, and serves them to friends. • Repeats back-and-forth rolling motion with clay to produce a long, snake-like shape.	• Makes a dough pancake by using a wood block as a press. • Uses a strainer or garlic-press to make "hair" out of dough and presses it onto a ball to make a person's head. • Using a rolling pin to flatten dough, communicates, "I'm making tortillas like my grandma." • Rolls out play dough into long strings, cuts them shorter with a plastic knife, and says, "These are noodles."
2.4 Begin to use paper and other materials to assemble simple collages.	**2.4** Use paper and other materials to make two- and three-dimensional assembled works.
Examples	**Examples**
• Glues leaves and other natural materials on a recycled paper bag. • Uses pieces of tissue paper and fabric to create a collage on a scrap of wallpaper.	• Uses dough and twigs to make and decorate a cake. • Uses pipe cleaners to create animal shapes. • Cuts colorful paper into long strips, twists the strips into wavy shapes, glues them to paper, and says, "These are ocean waves." • Shows the teacher and other children how to make an origami fish.†

*Roti is a traditional flatbread common in India and Pakistan. Like many breads around the world, *roti* is a staple accompaniment to other foods.

†Origami is a favorite Japanese and Chinese craft activity in which paper is folded to create shapes and objects.

2.0 Develop Skills in Visual Art (Continued)

At around 48 months of age	At around 60 months of age
2.5 Begin to recognize and name materials and tools used for visual arts.*	**2.5** Recognize and name materials and tools used for visual arts.*
Examples	**Examples**
• Sees finger paint on the table and asks the teacher, "Can I paint?" • Brings sparkly markers to the preschool program, shows them to other children, and explains why he likes them. • Points to an object on teacher's desk and says, "Hey, that's made out of dough!" • Tells the teacher, "This glue stick is not working! Can you give me another one?"	• Asks a friend, "Can I use the easel when you are done?" • Communicates, "That's my paintbrush. Yours is over there." • Asks the teacher, "Can we use glitter paint today?"
2.6 Demonstrate some motor control when working with visual arts tools.*	**2.6** Demonstrate increasing coordination and motor control when working with visual arts tools.*
Examples	**Examples**
• Draws on a sheet of paper without drawing off the edges of the paper. • Cuts lines in paper using child-sized scissors. • A child who is visually impaired colors within his space as defined by the use of a tray or placemat.	• Controls a crayon well enough to connect a line and complete a shape or circle. • Cuts sharp corners in paper. • While painting at an easel, repositions a paintbrush to keep the paint from dripping.

*Children who do not use oral language can indicate their recognition of materials and tools by touching the named implement when asked or indicating that an adult has pointed to the named item.

3.0 Create, Invent, and Express Through Visual Art

At around 48 months of age	At around 60 months of age
3.1 Create art and sometimes name the work.	**3.1** Intentionally create content in a work of art.
Examples	**Examples**
• Paints an entire piece of paper dark blue, dots the background with some white glue, and says, "This is the sky at night." • Cuts and tapes pieces of paper together and communicates, "It's a rocket ship."	• Molds a person out of dough, making a ball for the head. • Draws two human figures and tells a simple story about them. • Paints a picture of flowers and says, "We have a lot of these in our garden."
3.2 Begin to draw figures or objects.*	**3.2** Draw more detailed figures or objects with more control of line and shape.*
Examples	**Examples**
• Draws airplanes of various shapes and sizes on a piece of paper. • Uses horizontal swipes in blue finger paint to make an ocean or lake. • Paints a large blotch on paper and calls it "spilled juice."	• Draws a round figure with stick legs, hair, and facial features. • Draws a house or building, adding details such as a door, windows, or flowers in the front. • Draws an object from inside own home: for example, a toy car. • Communicates to another child, "Look! I drew my cat, Rosy."
3.3 Begin to use intensity of marks and color to express a feeling or mood.	**3.3** Use intensity of marks and color more frequently to express a feeling or mood.
Examples	**Examples**
• Child communicates, "I want to make a sun with lots of yellow tissue 'cause it's a happy day and we can play outside!" • After being read *Going On a Bear Hunt,* child uses dark paint at the easel and says (or communicates), "I'm on a bear hunt, and I'm not afraid."	• Child presses down firmly with marker, rubbing to create a wild thing after being read *Where the Wild Things Are.* • Uses heavy jagged, jumbled strokes in a finger painting of a rainstorm.

*Many examples describe the child drawing or manipulating objects or developing coordination and motor control. Children with motor impairments may need assistance from an adult or peer to manipulate objects in order to do things such as draw, paint, sculpt, tear, or color.

Music

1.0 Notice, Respond, and Engage*

At around 48 months of age	At around 60 months of age
1.1 Sustain attention and begin to reflect verbally about music; demonstrate familiarity with words that describe music.	**1.1** Verbally reflect on music and describe music by using an expanded vocabulary.
Examples	**Examples**
• Selects the book *Ben's Trumpet* and says, "I can play the horn just like they do at the Zigzag Club." • Picks up a music triangle and communicates, "I can make it ring three times." • Communicates, "I'm playing the drum." • Asks for the pair of maracas during singing and dance time.†	• Communicates, "That sounds just like "Happy Birthday to You" when teacher introduces the song "Good Morning to You." • Imitates tooting a horn or bowing a violin. • Demonstrates or says, "I'm the conductor." • Communicates, "I know that song; that's the one my grandma sings to me," after hearing the first few seconds of a compact disc (CD).
1.2 Recognize simple repeating melody and rhythm patterns.**	**1.2** Demonstrate more complex repeating melody and rhythm patterns.**
Examples	**Examples**
• Lifts head up and down, matching tones that go up and down. • Sings "'Happy Birthday' to me" while washing hands. • Taps slowly to one song and quickly to another, following the beat. • Marches in place during storytime to the beat of "The Ants Go Marching."	• Responds to tempo changes while listening to music by tapping, drumming, or clapping to the tempo and rhythm. • Accentuates the musical quality of the word *hello* by extending "oooo" and lowering pitch. • Sings and or claps with B-I-N-G-O song appropriately.

*Children who are deaf or hard of hearing will not notice, respond, or engage with music in the same way as peers who hear music. They may respond to vibrations, certain tones, or volume.

†Maracas are heard in many forms of Latin music and are also used in pop and classical music. They are characteristic of the music of Cuba, Puerto Rico, Colombia, Venezuela, Mexico, Jamaica, and Brazil.

**Children with motor impairments may not be able to repeat precise patterns.

1.0 Notice, Respond, and Engage *(Continued)*

At around 48 months of age	*At around 60 months of age*
1.3 Identify the sources of a limited variety of musical sounds.	**1.3** Identify the sources of a wider variety of music and music-like sounds.
Examples	**Examples**
• Begins to name sources of musical sounds, such as a piano, a CD player, or a wind-up toy. • Hears the marching band while playing on the playground and communicates, "I hear music coming from over there."	• Plays with some accuracy games about naming instruments. • Identifies the drum on the radio or a piano in the next room as the sound source hidden from view. • Listens to music and communicates, "That sounds like my dad's guitar."
1.4 Use body movement freely to respond loosely to beat—loud versus quiet (dynamics)—and tempo.*	**1.4** Use body movement freely and more accurately to respond to beat, dynamics, and tempo of music.*
Examples	**Examples**
• Responds to differing loudness or beat of a piano through bodily movements, not verbally. • Marches in a parade around the play yard with other children playing percussion instruments, although not in step with the beat.	• Communicates, "I'm tiptoeing because the music sounds quiet." • Happily dances to the rhythms of *merengue* or *salsa*.† • Accurately responds, with arm movements, to beat and tempo of a song played on the piano and anticipates continuing the beat and tempo.

*Children who are deaf or hard of hearing will not notice, respond, or engage with music in the same way as peers who hear music. They may respond to vibrations, certain tones, or volume. Children with motor impairments may not be able to respond precisely.

†*Merengue* and *salsa* are types of dance and music that are popular in Latin America and throughout the world. *Merengue* is from the Dominican Republic, and *salsa* is from Cuba.

2.0 Develop Skills in Music

At around 48 months of age	At around 60 months of age
2.1 Begin to discriminate between different voices and certain instrumental and environmental sounds. Follow words in a song.	**2.1** Become more able to discriminate between different voices and various instrumental and environmental sounds. Follow words in a song.
Examples	**Examples**
• Hears father's voice outside the classroom door and communicates, "My papa's here!" • When given metal instruments (triangle, bells) and small wooden instruments (rhythm sticks, wood block), can often identify them as sounding the same or different. • Puts seashell to ear and communicates, "It sounds like the ocean." • Communicates, "I hear a fire truck" during outside time and points to the road.	• After hearing the teacher read aloud a book in the different voices of the characters, says, "Read it again. Use your funny voice!" • Responds appropriately to a "sound lotto" game. • When metal instruments are struck (triangle, bells) and compared with small wooden instruments (rhythm sticks, wood block), can identify the sounds reliably as the same or different.
2.2 Explore vocally; sing repetitive patterns and parts of songs alone and with others.	**2.2** Extend vocal exploration; sing repetitive patterns and entire songs alone and with others in wider ranges of pitch.
Examples	**Examples**
• Sings a familiar children's song in its entirety, although the tune may be recognizable in only some places. • Delights in singing own song. • Hums the tune of a familiar song while at the play dough table. • Sings "De Colores" while holding hands with other children and swinging body from side to side.	• Sings during circle time a familiar children's song in its entirety with a recognizable tune. • Sings along with a group following the tune on the CD. • Sings solo in dramatic play area while holding a pretend microphone (for example, made of a paper towel roll).

3.0 Create, Invent, and Express Through Music

At around 48 months of age	*At around 60 months of age*
3.1 Explore vocal and instrumental skills and use instruments to produce simple rhythms and tones.	**3.1** Continue to apply vocal and instrumental skills and use instruments to produce more complex rhythms, tones, melodies, and songs.
Examples	**Examples**
• Grins and sings simple finger play songs, such as the "Itsy, Bitsy Spider." • Sings fragments of songs during daily activities, such as the first verse of "The Wheels on the Bus." • Explores rhythm instruments, such as rhythm sticks, drums, or shakers. • Enjoys singing into microphone.	• Participates in more complicated singing games: for example, portrays a character or object in a song, such as the animals in "Old MacDonald." • Sings many favorite songs in their entirety. • Uses and even "invents" rhythm instruments, such as a rhythm stick, drums, or shakers, to play along with songs during music time.
3.2 Move or use body to demonstrate beat and tempo, often spontaneously.	**3.2** Move or use body to demonstrate beat, tempo, and style of music, often intentionally.
Examples	**Examples**
• Rocks head side to side, initiating a certain beat or rhythm pattern. • Claps appropriately when singing, "If you're happy and you know it . . ." • Uses appropriate movement (for example, hand clapping, foot stomping, and bouncing) that reflects the energy level and pace of the music.	• Puts on a shawl and shows a friend how she danced for the kindergartners yesterday. • Sways to waltz music. • Leads the group by playing a quiet, steady beat on the drum or triangle. • Shows a friend a dance move from a dance he learned last weekend.
3.3 Improvise vocally and instrumentally.	**3.3** Explore, improvise, and create brief melodies with voice or instrument.
Examples	**Examples**
• Begins to play with songs, changing melody, adding words, or changing words. • Mimics and explores variations of familiar songs.	• Makes up own words to familiar tunes when singing in the dramatic play area. • During choice time, takes a xylophone from the music shelf to play a made-up song.

Drama

1.0 Notice, Respond, and Engage

At around 48 months of age	At around 60 months of age
1.1 Demonstrate an understanding of simple drama vocabulary.*	**1.1** Demonstrate a broader understanding of drama vocabulary.*
Examples	**Examples**
• Playing in the dramatic play area, communicates to another child, "You be the baby, I'll be the mommy, and we'll pretend the baby's sick." • While pretending to be horses in the teacher-led story dramatization, says, "We're using our imaginations." • Drapes a large box with a blanket. Says, "This can be the bear's house for our drama."	• Tells the teacher, "My favorite character is Big Anthony," or "I like the actor who was Big Anthony." • Draping yarn around two chairs, says, "This can be the spider web scenery for our Itsy Bitsy Spider drama." • While draping herself with colorful fabric in front of a mirror, says to another child, "I'm making my Rainbow Crow costume."
1.2 Identify preferences and interests related to participating in drama.	**1.2** Explain preferences and interests related to participating in drama.
Examples	**Examples**
• Talks like Papa Bear after seeing the teacher play this role in the story dramatization. • Pretends to be "baby bird" looking for his mama, recreating a favorite part of a story dramatization. • Takes a cape from the dress-up area and says, "I want to be Little Red Riding Hood."	• Communicates excitedly to her parent at pick-up time, "We pretended to be horses today in drama, and my horse climbed to the top of a mountain and played in the snow." • After a story dramatization, tells the teacher, "I liked being a Wild Thing because we got to be really wild!" • After pretending to be a goat in a dramatization of *The Three Billy Goats Gruff,* communicates to the teacher: "I didn't like it when you pretended to be the troll. You scared me!"

*Children communicating through an alternative language or communication system will need access to drama vocabulary (sign language, picture cards, and so on) with the appropriate terms.

1.0 Notice, Respond, and Engage (Continued)

At around 48 months of age	At around 60 months of age
1.3 Demonstrate knowledge of simple plot of a participatory drama.	**1.3** Demonstrate knowledge of extended plot and conflict of a participatory drama.
Examples	**Examples**
• Contributes to the ending of the drama: "Maybe all the animals are friends with each other at the end, and we could pretend to have an animal party." • Asks the teacher, "Can we do a drama about Doña Flor? We can pretend to be the people in the village, and you could pretend to be Doña Flor." • Using hand made props and a wolf puppet, reenacts a story from a book with a friend. Asks another child, "Where do the wolves go next?" The child replies, "Into the cave over there (pointing under a table)." • Pretending to be in a storm, contributes meaningful dialogue: One child says, "Help, help! The wind is blowing me in the water!" Another child replies: "Hold onto this rope and we'll pull you out." The first child says: "You saved me!"	• When the teacher asks what will happen next, child responds, "Our boat gets stuck and we have to scuba-dive under the water to fix it." • When asked to recall their dramatization of the story "Two Kingdoms," retells the drama sequentially. "First we went to Japan and saw Brother Moon and Sister Sun. Brother Moon was angry 'cause everybody liked Sister Sun more. He chased her in a cave, and everybody got cold. We made a dance for Sister Sun, and she came out to see us; everybody was warm and happy." • Contributes to resolving conflict in a drama: "We can help the woodcutter find another job, like getting honey from the bees and selling the honey. Then he won't have to cut the Kapok tree down." • Remembers a story and revises and extends the story plot, adding new characters. Says, "This time let's make the animals try to knock down the woodcutter's house, but he gives us bubblegum and our teeth get stuck together."

2.0 Develop Skills to Create, Invent, and Express Through Drama

At around 48 months of age	At around 60 months of age
2.1 Demonstrate basic role-play skills with imagination and creativity.	**2.1** Demonstrate extended role-play skills with increased imagination and creativity.
Examples	**Examples**
• Communicates to another child during a story dramatization: "You be the mommy, and I'll be the pizza man. And you tell me what you want on your pizza." • Imitates the movement of a squirrel running, stopping, and looking for an acorn. • Recreates the role of the cap seller, imitating the teacher's story dramatization. • Creates dialogue when improvising with other children in a role. Pretending to be a parrot, says to a friend pretending to be a tiger: "These are my baby parrots!" The friend, pretending to be a tiger says, "Want to see my baby tigers?" • Uses a squeaky voice and crawls on the floor to portray a hungry caterpillar.	• Changes voice and physical characteristics to portray the character of Max, then changes to a "Wild Thing" while extending the events of *Where the Wild Things Are*. • Incorporates problems and problem-solving skills in own drama scenarios with peers: with another friend, acts out a disagreement between a zoo-keeper and child who wants to keep monkey as a pet. • Creates an extended sequence of dialogue when improvising with peers in a role. One child, acting as a tiger says, "Let's hide the woodcutter's ax!" Another child acting as parrot says, "He can buy another one." Tiger: "I'm a tiger, I can eat him up!" Parrot: That's not nice. Let's jump down from a tree and scare him away. Tiger: "Okay! " • Recreates the roles from *The Three Billy Goats Gruff,* saying: "This is the bridge. You be the ugly troll, and I'll be the biggest Billy Goat. Ready? I'm going to cross the bridge."*
2.2 Add props and costumes to enhance dramatization of familiar stories and fantasy play with peers.	**2.2** Create and use an increasing variety of props, costumes and scenery to enhance dramatization of familiar stories and fantasy play with peers.
Examples	**Examples**
• Communicates, "Will you tie this on my back to make my wings?" • During outdoor play, sets up a carwash using buckets, water, and rags to wash tricycles. • Wraps a long piece of fabric around herself, pretending it is a *sari,* and does a few steps of Indian dance.† • Communicates, "These pinecones are going to be our eggs. We can use this sheet to make our nest."	• Puts plastic carrots and potatoes under brown fabric to make a vegetable garden. • Makes caves and animal nests by draping fabric over chairs and blocks. • Uses big blocks to make a boat, putting pillows inside for beds and a basket of smaller blocks inside for food. • Tapes small objects to a large box and asks a teacher to cut windows in it to make a spaceship.

*The Three Billy Goats Gruff is a popular Scandinavian story, with the signature folktale character of the troll. A troll is a fearsome member of a group of creatures from Norse mythology and Nordic literature, art, and music.
†A *sari* or *saree* is a female garment in the Indian subcontinent. A *sari* is a strip of cloth that is draped over the body in various styles.

Dance

1.0 Notice, Respond, and Engage*

At around 48 months of age	At around 60 months of age
1.1 Engage in dance movements.	**1.1** Further engage and participate in dance movements.
Examples	**Examples**
• Swirls a scarf or streamer with a back-and-forth hand movement outside. • Hops while listening to music. • Runs to join a group of children playing freeze dance. • Uses scarves to imitate ocean waves on hearing soft music played in class.	• Turns and bows as music ends. • Demonstrates a favorite dance to friends. • Demonstrates to other children in the program a dance she recently learned. • Holds a thick piece of paper like a fan, demonstrates a few steps of a fan dance by moving the fan back and forth and up and down. Twirls and stops.†
1.2 Begin to understand and use vocabulary related to dance.	**1.2** Connect dance terminology with demonstrated steps.
Examples	**Examples**
• Uses dance terms, such as *jump* and *spin*. • Responds to instructions using technical terms such as *bow* or *skip* (typically just learning to skip).	• Leaps, skips, runs, gallops, hops, slides, or jumps as directed by a song. • Begins to learn additional technical terms, such as *bend* and *straight*. • Communicates, "Look, I'm marching, to the Alphabet March."
1.3 Respond to instruction of one skill at a time during movement, such as a jump or fall.	**1.3** Respond to instruction of more than one skill at a time in movement, such as turning, leaping, and turning again. Often initiate a sequence of skills.
Examples	**Examples**
• Waves scarves in circles when music is playing. • Hops but cannot follow a planned movement pattern while hopping.	• Spins around in a circle waving scarves, jumps up in the air, and collapses on the ground. • Leaps four times and ends up at the starting point. • Jumps outdoors over a beam, spins, and falls. Asks a friend, "Can you do that?"

*Children communicating through an alternative language or communication system will need access to drama vocabulary (sign language, picture cards, and so on) with the appropriate terms.
†Fan dances are popular among Vietnamese, Korean, and Chinese children.

1.0 Notice, Respond, and Engage *(Continued)*

At around 48 months of age	*At around 60 months of age*
1.4 Explore and use different steps and movements to create or form a dance.	**1.4** Use understanding of different steps and movements to create or form a dance.
Examples	**Examples**
• Jumps and then spins when asked to "try a dance." • Stretches slowly upward while walking to a familiar song.	• Runs, stops and bends, and runs to demonstrate a dance. • Arches back like a cat and then pounces toward the mouse. • Creates different body movements when prompted to "dance like a thunderstorm" or "dance like a baby kitty."

2.0 Develop Skills in Dance

At around 48 months of age	At around 60 months of age
2.1 Begin to be aware of own body in space.	**2.1** Continue to develop awareness of body in space.
Examples	**Examples**
• Moves arms to music while seated and quickly pulls arms closer to body when they hit the arm of the chair. • Begins to apply developing motor skills, such as control and coordination of arms and of balance, to dance activities. • Leaps over a small object. • Selects appropriate place in circle by extending elbows to measure available personal space.	• Asks for wheelchair to be moved away from the wall when moving arms to music. • Demonstrates increasing control and coordination of movements; maintains balance through movements. • Performs a leap, not over an object.
2.2 Begin to be aware of other people in dance or when moving in space.	**2.2** Show advanced awareness and coordination of movement with other people in dance or when moving in space.
Examples	**Examples**
• Understands basic spatial relationships in movement (toward versus away, low versus high, big versus small, forward versus backward). • Shows beginning awareness of others when moving in a group (for example, not bumping into people). • Moves in relationship to others: beside, behind, in front of, away from (but prefers to be first or in front).	• Shows advanced understanding of basic spatial relationships in movement (toward versus away, low versus high, big versus small, forward versus backward) and brief combinations of movements (forward and high). • Shows full awareness of moving through a large group (for example, moves in space without bumping into people). • Dances in and identifies clear spatial relationships to other children: beside, behind, in front of, toward, and away from.
2.3 Begin to respond to tempo and timing through movement.	**2.3** Demonstrate some advanced skills in responding to tempo and timing through movement.
Examples	**Examples**
• Copies a simple rhythmic pattern as body movement with adult guidance (for example, clap-stomp). • Moves slow and fast to slow and fast music. • Begins to identify beat and respond to changes or differences in beat.	• Copies a more complex rhythmic pattern of body movement with adult guidance (clap-stomp-stomp). • Shows increasing ability to interpret music tempo in movement. Senses different tempi and adjusts movement accordingly. • Identifies beat and responds to changes or differences in beat.

3.0 Create, Invent, and Express Through Dance

At around 48 months of age	At around 60 months of age
3.1 Begin to act out and dramatize through music and movement patterns.	**3.1** Extend understanding and skills for acting out and dramatizing through music and movement patterns.
Examples	**Examples**
• Becomes a turtle and crawls on the floor. • Sings a favorite song about a duck while moving like a duck. • While listening to the Chinese song "Chong Chong Fei" (Little Bugs Flying), flaps arms up and down and runs in circles.	• Spontaneously moves to music and becomes an animal—turning swinging arms into an elephant's trunk. • Giggles and spins around and says, "Hey, the wind is blowing me like a leaf." • Dances silently across the room to wind-like sounds coming from the CD player. • Communicates, "I'm the wind."
3.2 Invent dance movements.	**3.2** Invent and recreate dance movements.
Examples	**Examples**
• While dancing, strikes a pose and then jumps. • Invents dance that may not appear to have typical dance movements. • Catches the ball and then does a "happy dance."	• Repeats the arm-swinging motion just invented while dancing. • Asks best friend to "try this arm dance."
3.3 Improvise simple dances that have a beginning and an end.	**3.3** Improvise more complex dances that have a beginning, middle, and an end.
Examples	**Examples**
• Dances story of going to pick flowers. • Dances story of building a doghouse for a new puppy. • Dances like a jet plane flying and landing.	• Makes up a dance of going to the ocean, swimming, getting cold, and returning home. • Dances like a wolf blowing a straw house down. • Dresses up in a long skirt and dances *folklorico* with peers in the same way as her cousins danced last weekend.
3.4 Communicate feelings spontaneously through dance and begin to express simple feelings intentionally through dance when prompted by adults.	**3.4** Communicate and express feelings intentionally through dance.
Examples	**Examples**
• Walks in exaggerated steps to march-type music. • Dances as mother with a caring expression comforting baby. • Does a little dance and communicates, "I'm happy, happy, happy!"	• Circles slowly with a stealthy movement, indicating she is a cat trying to catch a mouse. • Dances as the baker in the village while using facial expression and mixing movements to show what the baker does.

Bibliographic Notes

Visual Arts

A review of state standards for early learning in the visual arts suggests four principles:

1. Children express feelings, ideas, interests, stories, or moods through art. All children, including children with special needs, receive social and emotional benefits from being able to express themselves through visual art. The nonverbal aspect of visual art also gives English learners a powerful means to express themselves.
2. Children grow in abilities and show interest in different media such as crayons, paints, construction paper, and clay.
3. Children attend to and share opinions about their own and others' artwork.
4. Children progress in their ability to make detailed or realistic representations.

Research in the Visual Arts

A review of the research on children's development of drawing skills indicates the following finding:

> Generally, children continue to move through age and stage benchmarks, beginning with scribbles and progressing to representation and realism (Kellogg 1969; Matthews 1994).

> Just what is this progression of stages like? All individuals begin with simple outlined figures, such as circles and rectangles, which emerge as figures against grounds. Then they shift to figures whose structures are ordered in terms of maximum contrast—that is, all parts in these figures are laid out to highlight the distinction between horizontal and vertical planes: every part of the figures must be maximally discriminable from every other (Gardner 1980, 255).

There is a substantial body of research in preschool visual art development. Certain patterns emerge across the literature. In a classic work that remains relevant today, Schaefer-Simmern (1948) observed that young children growing up in different environments show similar developmental steps in expressing themselves through visual art. The following statements illustrate how a single visual form, the mandala (see the Glossary for a definition), is commonly seen at a certain stage.

> By the end of a child's third year, various "aggregations"—combined forms—often appear, like sun shapes, or circles divided into quarters or eighths, like a pie, which is called a mandala (Gardner 1980, 115).

> At the time of the mandala's [circle with crossed lines] appearance—somewhere near the end of the third year of life—the child is beginning to understand the representational nature of drawing (Gardner 1980, 53).

The following statements describe children's development in the creation of three-dimensional art.

> Very young children's first experience of clay is sensory, like their first finger-painting experiences. They delight in the process and the feeling of working with clay and discover its properties and how these can be used for expressive purposes (Clemens 1991 as cited in Wright 2003, 173).

While children are creating clay works and telling stories with clay ... they acquire a language of hands (Kolbe 2001, 22).

Music

Research shows that children typically develop musical skills and concepts in a predictable sequence. All young children, including children with special needs, acquire musical understandings and communication skills. They "progress developmentally from active, hands-on experiences, to meaningful pictorial representation, and finally to [more] . . . symbolic representations of sound ideas" (Andress 1998, 19).

Preschoolers are able to reproduce phrases of songs they hear, recognize a melody, and gain some understanding of pitch when exposed to instrumental music instruction (Shuter-Dyson and Gabriel 1981). Older preschool children are able to discriminate high and low registers of pitch and fast and slow tempos. They can tap simple rhythms. Their movement and rhythmic skills also show sequential development. Movement and rhythmic activity become more complex and purposeful as the preschool child develops. Preschool children become increasingly reflective about their own performances and are able to coordinate physical and vocal skills.

Auditory Skills

Hearing is one of the first senses to develop in humans. Younger preschoolers organize, reflect about, and respond to sound. Children are able to chant, imitate speech patterns, keep a steady beat, and demonstrate their perceptions through body movement. Children move from auditory discrimination, or the ability to recognize patterns of same and different sounds, to categorizing, organizing, and labeling what they hear. Children who are deaf or hard of hearing often respond to the beat of the music as it vibrates through the floor or is loud enough to be felt.

Vocal Abilities and the Development of Singing

Musical babble begins at about six months of age. From the onset of language, toddlers are spontaneous singers. By preschool, the child becomes more rhythmically and melodically accurate. However, singing in tune from phrase to phrase is inconsistent (Scott-Kassner 1993). Accuracy continues to increase, and drifting inadvertently to new keys decreases by age five or six. These changes are due, in part, to physical development of vocal chords and tissue. The child gradually gains control of her voice to use it expressively and in tune (Jordan-Decarbo and Nelson 2002).

Song Acquisition

Preschool children are drawn to songs with simple, short melodies and repeating melodic and rhythmic patterns (Jarjisian 1983). Preschool children like and learn songs they think are funny. "Instruction in singing for preschool children means singing to them, with them, and for them . . . the preschool years are the ones when language skills are developing rapidly; singing skills, another form of language, should develop as well" (McDonald and Simons 1989, 89).

Movement and Rhythmic Skills

Younger preschoolers produce a variety of coordinated movements to music, but as the toddler becomes a preschooler, his movements tend to be more purposeful, repetitious, and limited in variety. Movements are already complex and dance-like at around 48 months of age, as the spontaneous movement of the younger preschooler fades and attempts to coordinate with musical rhythm through clapping or tapping increase. Children at these ages are capable of responding to tempo changes in the music, but their movements rarely coordinate with the beat (Moog 1976).

Instruments and the Creation of Music

Experimenting with instruments captivates preschool children's imagination, and they enjoy their own ability to control sound. As children gain access to instruments, they discover the inherent sound possibilities of instruments, as well as their own capacities to control, refine, and express musical ideas (Moorhead, Sandvik, and Wight 1951). With encouragement, they may express their musical ideas in their own notation, using invented pictures or symbols. Preschool children also have increased positive social interactions with other children during musical play over time (Humpal 1991).

Listening

Preschoolers increasingly display the capacity and motivation to attend to excerpts of recorded music and classical music videos. Children especially enjoy listening to songs and music from their home culture and language. Instrumental music can serve as a bridge to literacy and language development when the music tells a story. Preschool children enjoy the active use of puppets and props and hearing instrumental music with stories. When exposed to different types, styles, or tonalities of music, they are attentive and open to new experiences, especially with active teacher encouragement (Nardo 1996).

Drama

Preschool children love to pretend to be characters, to be involved in dramatic situations, and to make believe with others. This can be called imaginary play, pretend play, or dramatic play. Like dramatic play, drama is experiential in nature, involving imagination, imitation, and a "living-through" quality that engages the whole child. During the preschool period, the main activities in drama are spontaneous or teacher-led role play and the enactment of pretend scenarios, not the formal staging of theatre works. Early skills in role playing, character understanding, and acting out are the foundations of the dramatic and theatre arts.

Pretending to be someone or to be doing something lies at the heart of children's play. Heathcote summarized 50 years of guiding the dramatic explorations of teachers and their children this way:

> Dramatizing makes it possible to isolate an event or to compare one event with another, to look at events that have happened to other people in other places and times perhaps, or to look at one's own experience after the event, within the safety of knowing that just at this moment it is not really happening. We can, however, feel that it is happening because drama uses the same rules we find in life. People exist in their environment, living a moment at a time and making those decisions which seem reasonable in the light of their present knowledge about

the current state of affairs. . . . So drama can be a kind of playing at or practice of living, tuning up those areas of feeling-capacity and expression-capacity as well as social-capacity (Heathcote 1975, 90).

Heathcote joins many other child development researchers who point out the importance of play in children's growing awareness of the world and understanding of the nature of the people, things, and situations they encounter (Gardner 1973; Fein 1981). The primary source of this growing awareness is children's cultural and linguistic experience with their families and communities.

Drama and Learning

Research studies in classroom drama and dramatic play mainly address the implications for various aspects of growth and development rather than the development of particular skills. Podlozny (2000) produced a comprehensive assessment of learning through drama, a synthesis of 80 studies published during the previous 30 years. This review indicates that classroom drama can foster development in spoken language in a variety of ways. Dramatic play is associated with gains in story understanding, oral language skills, and reading-readiness at around ages four and five, across multiple research studies. Because of the value of drama and dramatic play, it is important for teachers to adapt and create opportunities for children with special needs to participate fully in this type of learning.

Drama and Social Development

Studies also address the effects of dramatic play and enactment on children's social development. Dramatizing is often very social. For example, when pretending to be a teacher, a child needs children to teach. Through drama, children find out not only what it means to *be* or *do* something in a pretend situation, but also begin to perceive their actions in the light of the actions of others in the play. They put themselves in the shoes of another character and can come away with a growing understanding of the behavior and motivation of other people. Acting out situations from stories, such as demonstrating empathy or resolving a conflict through negotiation, can supply a child with some social skills, an opportunity to practice and experience a different way of interacting (Catterall 2007).

Basic Skills in Drama

Research in dramatic play does not generally focus on what might be called basic drama skills, or building blocks of dramatic expression such as, how well a child acts in pretending or in a dramatization, or how well a child organizes and designs his own or a group dramatic presentation. There are no major parallels in drama to the building-block skills in visual art, such as controlling a brushstroke, or in music, such as the ability to keep time with a shaker. The ground-level skills in drama for preschool children include basic verbal and movement skills.

Expert Practitioner Views of Drama and Young Children

The drama foundations are informed by the contributions of expert practitioners and research-informed drama practice in preschools. The work of Brown and Pleydell (1999) and that of Hereford and Shall (1991) were particularly influential. Hendy and Toon's (2001) work offers descriptions of drama behaviors and skills observed in children from age one to age six. Hyatt's (2006) work on connecting drama activities to children's books describes developmentally appropriate routines for preschool children.

Dance

We are born moving. Dance and movement are an inherent part of our lives and as natural as breathing. Dance is an elemental human experience and a means of expression. It begins before words are formed, and it is innate in children before they possess command over language. Movement is brought to the fore when thoughts or emotions are too overwhelming or cannot be expressed in words.

As described in the *Standards for Dance in Early Childhood* (National Dance Education Organization 2009), children move naturally. They move to get around and to express a thought or feeling; they move because it is joyful and comforting. They learn movement patterns as readily as they learn language. Like language, movement patterns are embedded in young children's cultural experiences. It is valuable to incorporate cultural ideas when supporting movement development with English learners. When movement becomes consciously structured and is performed with awareness, for its own sake, it becomes dance (Cone and Cone 2004).

Research suggests that formal dance instruction in early childhood has many potential benefits, such as increasing self-esteem, enhancing motor awareness and control, heightening coordination, and improving balance and confidence in movement (Faber 1994). Dance benefits the physical, mental, and emotional growth of the child (Reedy 2003). Children with special needs benefit from opportunities to experience pleasurable, self-directed movement unrelated to any therapeutic goals.

Regular dancing and dance instruction develop flexibility, coordination, sensitivity to music and rhythm, and kinetic self-expression (Laban 1971). The physical developments associated with dancing benefit the child's abilities to perform in other physical activities. Movements involved in dancing can serve to make and strengthen new connections in the brain. When the brain learns to respond to particular movements more efficiently, it becomes able to contribute to related physical tasks.[1]

Skill development in dance affects the child's self-image and develops self-confidence along with physical and spatial skills (Gerhardt 1973). These experiences enhance the child's intellectual, physical, and emotional growth (Paskevska 1997).

Parents have reported that their child's ability to learn and concentrate improves after they have started dance lessons (Stinson 1990). In the case of children with special needs, dance can be used to encourage movements that are part of therapeutic intervention, such as stretching, reaching, kicking, jumping, and leaping. When a child is not able to walk independently, dance can be accomplished through movement of the body. These types of movement activities help children with motor delays appreciate the ways in which their bodies move.

---

[1]General principles of learning transfer through brain plasticity, or rewiring, are discussed in Catterall (2005).

Dance Abilities of the Younger Preschooler

In all four of the principal art forms, including dance, children vary widely in their accomplishments and abilities. Each child has her own rate and own personal way of maturing and growing. Ames and Ilg (1976; 1985) and Mara (1987a, b, c, and d) describe the specific stages of development of dance skills relevant to children at around 48 and 60 months of age.

Movement is often a source of delight for preschool children. As postural control develops, the child can balance on tiptoes for a moment and can walk in a straight line, forward and backward. The younger preschooler has skills that enable her to notice and enjoy subtleties of movement. For example, she notices facial expressions, has a sense of direction, and can follow a target without losing attention (Ames and Ilg 1985; Destefanis and Firchow 2008). The younger preschooler can run, climb, cooperate with other children, and dress himself (somewhat). He no longer looks or acts as top-heavy as a toddler, and standing now requires little conscious effort. The child can easily maintain equilibrium with heels together, stand on one foot with momentary balance, and walk erect and swing arms in opposition, although the opposition skill is still developing. Preschool children can alternate feet when going up steps, but they may need to same-step on the way down. They can gallop and get up from a squatting position. Their hands are becoming more skillful and dexterous. For more information on physical development during preschool, please see "Foundations in Physical Development."

Dance Abilities of the Older Preschooler

The older preschool child, like the younger one, is often exuberant, energetic, and ready for anything. He tends to enjoy excitement and anything new or adventurous. Compared to the younger child, he is generally more self-directed and interested in gathering new information and perfecting old skills. Sharing and taking turns comes easier, and children enjoy cooperative play (Ames and Ilg 1976; Isenberg and Jalongo 2001).

The older preschool child can coordinate movements much better than a year earlier and can move effectively with a growing sense of balance. The child is able to do a running leap and follow spatial directions. The preschool child, at around 60 months of age, adds more technical dance terms to her vocabulary. At this age, children can initiate a brief dance sequence and depend less on teacher prompts or instructions to engage in expressive dance. Older preschool children are more interested and patient about observing dance presentations, either by dancers visiting the program or more-formal staged productions.

By around 60 months of age, children can typically coordinate and control more parts of the body into dance steps or routines and can work more effectively with others in moving through a dance space. At this age, children are more able to dance and move in time to music or percussion. Older preschool children are more inclined and able to create and perform dances that depict stories. They often invent dance moves and sequences of their own and are increasingly able to convey feelings and mood through dance.

Glossary

balance. A state of equilibrium referring to the balance of weight or the spatial arrangement of bodies.

beat. The beat or pulse in a piece of music is the regular rhythmic pattern of the music.

character. An imaginary person in a literary work, such as a play, a story, or a poem.

collage. From the French word *coller*, to glue. A work made by gluing materials, such as paper scraps, photographs, and cloth, to a flat surface.

content. The meaning or message contained and communicated by a work of art, including its emotional, intellectual, symbolic, thematic, and narrative connotations.

costume. Clothing or materials worn to depict a character. Preschool children often create their own costumes, using pieces of fabric and scarves.

dance. Movement selected and organized for aesthetic purposes, or as a medium of expression, rather than for its function as work or play.

dance sequence. The order in which a series of movements and shapes occurs.

dialogue. The conversation of characters in a literary work, such as a play, a story, or a poem.

drama. A participatory experience in which two or more children pretend to be someone else or to be someplace else. Drama is used in the preschool classroom as an experiential, play-based learning medium. Whereas theater is performance-oriented, drama at the preschool level is process-oriented and improvisational in nature. Generally guided by the teacher, children "live through" the drama, exploring and expressing their thoughts, feelings, and ideas. Teacher-led drama is similar to scaffolding in dramatic play, in the sense that the teacher's questioning supports the child's use of his or her imagination. For more information on the role of the teacher in drama, see the *California Preschool Curriculum Framework* (2010).

dramatizing. Creating and acting out pretend characters in imaginary or staged contexts.

dynamics. An element of musical expression relating to the degree of loudness or softness, or volume, of a sound.

enactment. See *dramatizing*.

environmental cue. An external instruction, as from a teacher, adult, or another child.

figure. Separate shape(s) distinguishable from a background or ground.

fine motor activity. A physical activity, such as using crayons, stacking blocks, or cutting with scissors, that uses the smaller muscle groups of primarily the fingers, hands, and wrists.

gross motor activity. A physical activity, such as throwing, striking, running, or jumping, that uses the major muscle groups of the arms, legs, and trunk.

image. A concrete representation of a sense impression, a feeling, or an idea.

kinetic self-expression. Expressing oneself through body movement.

locomotor movement. Projecting the body into or through space (from one place to another).

mandala. Sanskrit word for *circle*. Children commonly make mandalas, for example, by placing two sticks in an x formation and wrapping yarn around them. Or children may make a mandala in drawings that include a circle and crossed lines that may represent people or the sun.

melodically accurate. Conforming to the customary melody of a song.

melody. A succession of single tones or pitches perceived by the mind as a unity.

movement pattern. A repeated sequence of movement ideas, a rhythmic movement sequence, a spatial design on the floor or in the air, or a certain relationship or grouping of people.

note. A single sound or its representation in notation.

participatory drama. See *drama,* above. For preschool children, drama is participatory.

perspective. A system for creating an illusion of depth or three-dimensional space on a two-dimensional surface. The term usually refers to linear perspective, which is based on the fact that parallel lines or edges appear to converge and objects appear smaller as the distance between them and the viewer increases.

pitch. The pitch of a note is the frequency of its vibrations.

plot. The story line or sequence of events that make up a drama. The plot can evolve in an improvised drama.

props. The handheld articles or objects used during a dramatization. In drama for preschool children, nonrepresentational props are often used to engage children's imagination and skills in symbolic thinking. For example, when a child's imaginary bus breaks down, a child might use a box of bendable straws for tools instead of realistic tool-like toys.

representation. A creation that is a visual or tangible rendering of someone or something.

rhythm. The controlled movement of music in time.

rhythm pattern. A repeating pattern of beats and accents (loud and soft sounds) in music.

rhythmic skills. The abilities to recognize and/or reproduce repeating pattern of beats and accents (loud and soft sounds) in music.

role play. Changing one's behavior (voice, movement, or language use) to depict or act like another person, animal, or thing, imaginary or real. Extended role-play skills include more detail regarding change of voice, movement, language use, and the child's ability to maintain the character depiction longer. For example, children at around age three might be able to hold their physical depiction of an elephant for only a minute or two, while a child at around age four or five would be able to intentionally maintain the depiction longer.

scenario. An outline or synopsis of a series of actions or events that summarize the plot of the dramatization. In some drama work, the scenario is improvised, evolving from the ideas and suggestions of the participants. For example, the teacher may lead the children in an imaginary boat trip, asking the children what they see in the water or where they would like to go next, and integrate their ideas.

setting. The time and place of a literary work that establish its context.

story dramatization. A process in which children are invited to act out, extend, and/or change in some way a story that their teacher has shared. This type of drama is often led by the teacher-in-role, while children typically take on the role of the protagonist (main character). For example, in leading a story dramatization of *Where the Wild Things Are* by Maurice Sendak, the teacher may pretend to be Max's mother and all the children pretend to be Max, then later take on the role of Max, leading the children in "rumpus making" while they pretend to be the "Wild Things." Playing the protagonist facilitates the children's ability to step into the main character's shoes. (For more information on story dramatization, see the *California Preschool Curriculum Framework, Volume 3* [forthcoming]).

story understanding. Comprehending characters, actions, relationships, motivations, and setting in a story.

style. A characteristic manner of presentation of musical or dance elements (for example, melody, rhythm, harmony, dynamics, form, movement patterns, and costuming).

symbol. A form or image implying or representing something beyond its obvious and immediate meaning.

tempo. The speed of music or a dance.

temporal skills. Abilities and understanding related to time (for example, maintaining tempo in music and understanding the proportional nature of different musical notes such as quarter notes and half notes).

texture. The tactile quality of a surface or the representation or invention of the appearance of such a surface quality.

time. An element of music or dance involving rhythm, phrasing, tempo, accent, and duration. Time can be metered, as in music, or based on body rhythms, such as breath, emotions, and heartbeat.

tone. A sound of definite pitch.

visual arts tools. Implements, such as a paintbrush, easel, scissors, or sponge, for creating the marks, colors, textures, and shapes of visual art.

References and Source Materials

Visual Arts

Catterall, J. S., and K. Peppler. 2007. "Learning in the Visual Arts and the Worldviews of Young Children," *Cambridge Journal of Education (UK)*, Vol. 37, No. 4, 543–60.

Clemens, S. G. 1991. "Art in the Classroom: Making Every Day Special," *Young Children*, Vol. 46, No. 2, 4–11.

Gardner, H. 1980. *Artful Scribbles: The Significance of Children's Drawings.* New York: Basic Books.

Kellogg, R. 1969. *Analyzing Children's Art.* Palo Alto, CA: National Press Books.

Kelly, E., and J. McConville. 1998. *Art for the Very Young.* Grand Rapids, MI: Frank Schaffer Publications.

Kolbe, U. 1993. "Co-player and Co-artist: New Roles for the Adult in Children's Visual Arts Experiences," *Early Child Development and Care*, Vol. 90, No. 1, 73–82.

Kolbe, U. 2001. *Rapunzel's Supermarket: All About Young Children and Their Art.* Sydney, Australia: Peppinot Press.

Lowenfeld, V., and W. L. Brittain. 1987. *Creative and Mental Growth* (Eighth edition). New York: Macmillan.

Matthews, J. 1994. "Deep Structures in Children's Art: Development and Culture," *Visual Arts Research*, Vol. 20, No. 2, 29–50.

Matthews, J. 1997. "The 4-Dimensional Language of Infancy: The Interpersonal Basis of Art Practice," *Journal of Art and Design Education*, Vol. 16, No. 3, 285–93.

Mattil, E. L., and B. Marzan. 1981. *Meaning in Children's Art: Projects for Teachers.* Englewood Cliffs, NJ: Prentice-Hall.

National Association for the Education of Young Children (NAEYC) and the National Association of Early Childhood Specialists in State Departments of Education. 1991. "Guidelines for Appropriate Curriculum Content and Assessment in Programs Serving Children Ages 3 Through 8," *Young Children*, Vol. 46, No. 3, 21–38.

Piaget, J. 1953. "Art Education and Child Psychology," in *Education and Art: A Symposium.* Edited by E. Ziegfeld. Paris: United Nations Educational, Scientific, and Cultural Organization (UNESCO).

Raboff, E. 1987-1988. Art for Children series. New York: Harper-Collins.

Schaefer-Simmern, H. 1948. *The Unfolding of Artistic Activity: Its Basis, Processes, and Implications.* Berkeley, CA: University of California Press.

Schirrmacher, R. 2006. *Art and Creative Development for Young Children* (Fifth edition). Clifton Park, NY: Thomson Delmar Learning.

Seefeldt, C. 1995. "Art: A Serious Work," *Young Children*, Vol. 50, No. 3, 39–45.

Smith, N. R. 1982. "The Visual Arts in Early Childhood Education: Development and the Creation of Meaning," in *Handbook of Research in Early Childhood Education.* Edited by B. Spodek. New York: The Free Press.

Smith, N. R., and others. 1993. *Experience and Art: Teaching Children to Paint* (Second edition). New York: Teachers College Press.

Smith, R. A. 2000. "Policymaking for the Future: Three Critical Issues," *Arts Education Policy Review*, Vol. 102, No. 2, 21–22.

Visual and Performing Arts Content Standards for California Public Schools: Prekindergarten Through Grade Twelve. 2001. Sacramento: California Department of Education.

Wachowiak, F. 1985. *Emphasis Art: A Qualitative Art Program for Elementary and Middle Schools* (Fourth edition). New York: Harper and Row.

Woodford, S. 1983. *Looking at Pictures.* Cambridge, UK: Cambridge University Press.

Wright, S. 2003. *The Arts, Young Children, and Learning.* Boston: Allyn and Bacon.

Music

Andress, B. 1998. *Music for Young Children.* Orlando, FL: Harcourt Brace.

Burnett, M. 1988. *All About Me. I Like to Sing, Vol. 1.* Van Nuys, CA: Alfred Publishing.

Catterall, J. S., and F. H. Rauscher. 2008. "Unpacking the Impact of Music on Intelligence," in *Neurosciences and Music Pedagogy.* Edited by W. Gruhn and F. Rauscher. New York: Nova Science Publishers.

Davidson, L., and L. Scripp. 1989. "Education and Development in Music from a Cognitive Perspective," in *Children and the Arts.* Edited by D. Hargreaves. Philadelphia, PA: Open University Press.

Flohr, J. March 1984. Young Children's Improvisations: A Longitudinal Study. Paper presented at the Music Educators National Conference, Chicago, Illinois.

Forrai, K. 1990. *Music in Preschool* (Second edition). Translated by J. Sinor. Budapest: Corvina.

Getting in Tune: The Powerful Influence of Music on Young Children's Development. 2002. Edited by A. Lieberman and others. Washington, DC: Zero to Three (brochure).

Hargreaves, D. 1986. *The Developmental Psychology of Music.* Cambridge: Cambridge University Press.

Humpal, M. E. 1991. "The Effects of an Integrated Early Childhood Music Program on Social Interaction Among Children with Handicaps and Their Typical Peers," *Journal of Music Therapy,* Vol. 28, No. 3, 161–77.

Imberty, M. 1996. "Linguistic and Musical Development in Preschool and School-Age Children," in *Musical Beginnings: Origins and Development of Musical Competence.* Edited by I. Deliege and J. Sloboda. Oxford: Oxford University Press.

Jarjisian, C. 1983. "Pitch Pattern Instruction and the Singing Achievement of Young Children," *Psychology of Music,* Vol. 11, 19–25.

Jordan-DeCarbo, J., and J. Nelson. 2002. "Music in Early Childhood Education," in *The New Handbook of Research on Music Teaching and Learning.* Edited by R. Colwell and C. Richardson. New York: Oxford University Press.

McDonald, D. T., and G. M. Simons. 1989. *Musical Growth and Development: Birth Through Six.* New York: Schirmer Books.

Moog, H. 1976. *The Musical Experience of the Pre-school Child.* London: Schott Music Ltd.

Moorhead, G. E., and D. Pond. 1941. *Music of Young Children.* Santa Barbara, CA: Pillsbury Foundation for the Advancement of Music Education.

Moorhead, G. E., F. Sandvik, and D. Wight. 1951. *Music of Young Children, Vol. IV: Free Use of Music for Musical Growth.* Santa Barbara, CA: Pillsbury Foundation for Advancement of Music Education.

Music Educators National Conference. 1958. *Music for Fours and Fives: A Report.* Washington, DC: Music Educators National Conference.

Music Educators National Conference. 1985. *The Young Child and Music: Contemporary Principles in Child Development and Music Education.* Edited by J. Boswell. Reston, VA: Music Educators National Conference.

Music Educators National Conference. 1994. *Opportunity-to-Learn Standards for Music Instruction: Grades preK–12.* Reston, VA: Music Educators National Conference.

Music Educators National Conference Task Force for National Standards in the Arts. 1994. *The School Music Program: A New Vision: The K-12 National Standards, preK Standards, and What They Mean to Music Educators.* Reston, VA: Music Educators National Conference.

Music Educators National Conference Committee on Performance Standards. 1996. *Performance Standards for Music: Strategies and Benchmarks for Assessing Progress Toward the National Standards, Grades preK-12.* Reston, VA: Music Educators National Conference.

Nardo, R. 1996. California Survey of Music in Early Childhood: Teacher Preparation and the Role of the Community College. Los Angeles: University of Southern California (doctoral dissertation).

Pouthas, V. "The Development of the Perception of Time and Temporal Regulation of Action in Infants and Children," in *Musical Beginnings: Origins and Development of Musical Competence.* Edited by I. Deliege and J. Sloboda. Oxford: Oxford University Press.

Reilly, M. L., and L. F. Olson. 1985. *It's Time for Music: Songs and Lesson Outlines for Early Childhood Music.* Van Nuys, CA: Alfred Publishing.

Richards, M. H. 1984. *Aesthetic Foundations for Thinking-Rethought: Part 1, Experience.* Portola Valley, CA: Richards Institute of Music Education and Research.

Scott-Kassner, C. 1993. "Musical Characteristics," in *Music in Prekindergarten: Planning and Teaching.* Edited by M. Palmer and W. L. Sims. Reston, VA: Music Educators National Conference.

Shuter-Dyson, R., and C. Gabriel. 1981. *The Psychology of Musical Ability.* London: Methuen.

Sims, W. L. 1991. "Effects of Instruction and Task Format on Preschool Children's Music Concept Discrimination," *Journal of Research in Music Education,* Vol. 39, 298–310.

Drama

Bredekamp, S., and C. Copple, eds. *Developmentally Appropriate Practice in Early Childhood Programs Serving Children from Birth Through Age Eight.* 1987. Washington, DC: National Association for the Education of Young Children (NAEYC).

Brown, V., and S. Pleydell. 1999. *The Dramatic Difference: Drama in the Preschool and Kindergarten Classroom.* Portsmouth, NH: Heinemann.

Catterall, J. S. 2007. "Enhancing Peer Conflict Resolution Skills Through Drama: An Experimental Study," *Research in Drama Education,* Vol. 12, No. 2, 163–78.

Chafel, J. A. 1987. "Achieving Knowledge About Self and Others Through Physical Object and Fantasy Play," *Early Childhood Research Quarterly,* Vol. 2, 27–43.

Christie, J. 1982. "Sociodramatic Play Training," *Young Children,* Vol. 37, No. 4, 25–32.

Fein, G. 1981. "Pretend Play in Childhood: An Integrative Review," *Child Development,* Vol. 52, 1095–118.

Fink, R. S. 1976. "Role of Imaginative Play in Cognitive Development," *Psychological Reports,* Vol. 39, 895–906. As summarized in *Critical Links: Learning in the Arts and Student Academic and Social Development.* Edited by R. Deasy. Washington, DC: Arts Education Partnership.

Gardner, H. 1973. *The Arts and Human Development.* New York: John Wiley and Sons.

Goodman, J. R. 1990. A Naturalistic Study of the Relationship Between Literacy Development and Dramatic Play in Five-Year-Old Children. Nashville, TN: George Peabody College for Teachers (doctoral dissertation). As summarized in *Critical Links: Learning in the Arts and Student Academic and Social Development.* Edited by R. Deasy. Washington, DC: Arts Education Partnership.

Griffing, P. 1983. "Encouraging Dramatic Play in Early Childhood," *Young Children,* Vol. 38, No. 4, 13–22.

Heath, S. B.; E. Soep; and A. Roach. 1998. "Living the Arts Through Language and Learning: A Report on Community-Based Youth Organizations," *Americans for the Arts Monographs,* Vol. 2, No. 7, 1–20.

Heathcote, D. 1975. "Drama and Learning," in *Dorothy Heathcote: Collected Writings on Education and Drama.* Edited by L. Johnson and C. O'Neill. Cheltenham, England: Stanley Thomas Publishers.

Hendy, L., and Toon, L. 2001. *Supporting Drama and Imaginative Play in the Early Years.* Buckingham, UK: Open University Press.

Hereford, N. J., and J. Shall, eds. 1991. *Learning Through Play: Dramatic Play, A Practical Guide for Teaching Young Children.* New York: Scholastic.

Hiatt, K. 2006. *Drama Play: Bringing Books to Life Through Drama for 4-7 Year Olds.* Abingdon, UK: David Fulton Publishers.

Klugman, E., and S. Smilansky, eds. *Children's Play and Learning: Perspectives and Policy Implications.* 1990. New York: Teachers College Press.

Levy, A. K.; L. Schaefer; and P. C. Phelps. 1986. "Increasing Preschool Effectiveness: Enhancing the Language Abilities of Three- and Four-Year-Old Children Through Planned Sociodramatic Play," *Early Childhood Research Quarterly,* Vol. 1, No. 2, 133–40.

Mages, W. K. 2008. "Does Creative Drama Promote Language Development in Early Childhood? A Review of the Methods and Measures Employed in the Empirical Literature," *Review of Educational Research,* Vol. 78, No. 1, 124–52.

Miller, K. 1989. The Outside Play and Learning Book: Activities for Young Children. Mt. Rainier, MD: Gryphon House.

Monighan-Nourot, P.; B. Scales; and J. L. Van Hoorn. 1987. *Looking at Children's Play: A Bridge Between Theory and Practice.* New York: Teachers College Press.

Pellegrini, A. D. 1980. *Symbolic Functioning and Children's Early Writing: Relations Between Kindergartener's Play and Isolated Word Writing Fluency.* ED-201407. Athens, GA: University of Georgia. As summarized in *Critical Links: Learning in the Arts and Student Academic and Social Development.* Edited by R. Deasy. Washington, DC: Arts Education Partnership.

Pellegrini, A. D. 1984a. "Identifying Casual Elements in the Thematic-Fantasy Play Paradigm," *American Educational Research Journal,* Vol. 21, No. 3, 691–701. As summarized in *Critical Links: Learning in the Arts and Student Academic and Social Development.* Edited by R. Deasy. Washington, DC: Arts Education Partnership.

Pellegrini, A. D. 1984b. "The Effect of Dramatic Play on Children's Generation of Cohesive Text," *Discourse Processes,* Vol. 7, 57–67. As summarized in *Critical Links: Learning in the Arts and Student Academic and Social Development.* Edited by R. Deasy. Washington DC: Arts Education Partnership.

Pellegrini, A. D., and L. Galda. 1982. "The Effects of Thematic-Fantasy Play Training on the Development of Children's Story Comprehension," *American Educational Research Journal,* Vol. 19, No. 3, 443–52. As summarized in *Critical Links: Learning in the Arts and Student Academic and Social Development.* Edited by R. Deasy. Washington, DC: Arts Education Partnership.

Podlozny, A. Fall 2000. "Strengthening Verbal Skills Through the Use of Classroom Drama: A Clear Link," *Journal of Aesthetic Education,* Vol. 34, Nos. 3–4, 239–76.

Rooyackers, P. 1998. *101 Drama Games for Children: Fun and Learning with Acting and Make-Believe.* Alameda, CA: Hunter House, Inc.

Rowe, D. 1998. "The Literate Potentials of Book-Related Dramatic Play," *Reading Research Quarterly,* Vol. 33, No.1, 10–35.

Schraeder, C. 1990. "Symbolic Play as a Curricular Tool for Early Literacy Development," *Early Childhood Research Quarterly,* Vol. 5, No. 1., 79–103.

Segal, M. M., and Adcock, D. 1981. *Just Pretending: Ways to Help Children Grow Through Their Imaginative Play.* N.p.: Prentice Hall.

Segal, M. M., and Adcock, D. 1998. *Your Child at Play: Three to Five Years: Conversation, Creativity, and Learning Letters, Words, and Numbers* (Second edition). New York: New Market Press.

Seidel, S. 1999. "'Stand and Unfold Yourself.' A Monograph on the Shakespeare and Company Research Study," in *Champions of Change: The Impact of the Arts on Learning.* Edited by E. Fiske. Washington, DC: The Arts Education Partnership and The President's Committee on the Arts and Humanities.

Smilansky, S. 1990. *Facilitating Play: A Medium for Promoting Cognitive, Socio-Emotional and Academic Development in Young Children.* Gaithersburg, MD: Psychosocial and Educational Publications.

Tamburrini, J. 1974. "Play and Intellectual Development," *Paedagogica Europaea,* Vol. 9, No. 1, 51–59.

Toye, N., and F. Prendiville. 2000. *Drama and Traditional Story for the Early Years.* New York: Routledge Falmer.

Williamson, P. A., and S. B. Silvern. 1992. "'You Can't Be Grandma; You're a Boy': Events Within the Thematic Fantasy Play Context that Contribute to Story Comprehension," *Early Childhood Research Quarterly,* Vol. 7, No. 1, 75–93.

Wolfgang, C., and T. Sanders. 1981. "Defending Young Children's Play as the Ladder to Literacy," *Theory Into Practice,* Vol. 20, No. 2, 116–20.

Dance

Ames, L. B., and F. L. Ilg. 1976. *Your Four-Year-Old: Wild and Wonderful.* New York: Dell Publishing.

Ames, L. B., and F. L. Ilg. 1985. *Your Three-Year-Old: Friend or Enemy.* New York: Dell Publishing.

Anderson, J. 1986. *Ballet and Modern Dance: A Concise History.* Princeton, NJ: Princeton Book Company.

Catterall, J. S. 2002. "The Arts and the Transfer of Learning," in *Critical Links: Learning in the Arts and Student Academic and Social Development.* Edited by R. Deasy. Washington, DC: Arts Education Partnership.

Catterall, J. S. 2005. "Conversation and Silence: Transfer of Learning Through the Arts," *Journal for Learning Through the Arts,* Vol. 1, No.1, 1–12.

Children's Dance. 1973. Edited by G. A. Fleming. Washington, DC: American Association of Health, Physical Education, and Recreation Press.

Cone, T. P., and S. L. Cone. 2004. *Teaching Children Dance.* Champaign, IL: Human Kinetics, Inc.

Destefanis, J., and N. Firchow. 2008. *Developmental Milestones: Ages 3 Through 5,* in *Great Schools: Involved Parents, Successful Kids.* Originally developed by Schwab Learning/Schwab Learning Foundation. http://www.greatschools.net/cgi-vin/showarticle/2324 (accessed February 23, 2009).

Faber, R. 1994. The Primary Movers: Kinesthetic Learning for Primary School Children. Washington, DC: American University (master of arts thesis).

Gerhardt, L. A. 1973. *Moving and Knowing: The Young Child Orients Himself in Space.* Englewood Cliffs, NJ: Prentice Hall.

Great Schools: Involved Parents, Successful Kids. Originally developed by Schwab Learning/Schwab Learning Foundation. http://www.greatschools.net/cgi-bin/showarticle/2324 (accessed February 23, 2009).

Hammond, S. N. 1974. *Ballet Basics.* Palo Alto, CA: Mayfield Publishing Company.

Hammond, S. N. 1982. *Ballet: Beyond the Basics.* Palo Alto, CA: Mayfield Publishing Company.

Isenberg, J. P., and M. R. Jalongo. 2006. *Creative Thinking and Arts-Based Learning: Preschool Through Fourth Grade* (Fourth edition). Upper Saddle River, NJ: Merrill.

Laban, R. V. 1971. *The Mastery of Movement.* London: MacDonald and Evans.

Laws, K. 1984. *The Physics of Dance.* New York: Schirmer Books.

Mara, T. 1987a. *First Steps in Ballet: Basic Exercises at the Barre.* Princeton, NJ: Princeton Book Company.

Mara, T. 1987b. *Second Steps in Ballet: Basic Centre Exercises.* Princeton, NJ: Princeton Book Company.

Mara, T. 1987c. *Third Steps in Ballet: Basic Allegro Steps.* Princeton, NJ: Princeton Book Company.

Mara, T. 1987d. *Fourth Steps in Ballet: On Your Toes! Basic Pointe Work.* Princeton, NJ: Princeton Book Company.

National Dance Education Organization. 2009. *Standards for Dance in Early Childhood.* Bethesda, MD: National Dance Education Organization.

National Dance Education Organization. 2005a. *Standards for Learning and Teaching Dance in the Arts: Ages 5–18.* Bethesda, MD: National Dance Education Organization.

National Dance Education Organization. 2005b. *Professional Teaching Standards for Dance in the Arts Education.* Bethesda, MD: National Dance Education Organization.

Paskevska, A. 1981. *Both Sides of the Mirror: The Science and Art of Ballet.* Brooklyn, NY: Dance Horizons.

Paskevska, A. 1992. *Both Sides of the Mirror: The Science and Art of Ballet* (Second edition). Pennington, NJ: Princeton Book Company.

Paskevska, A. 1997. *Getting Started in Ballet: A Parent's Guide to Dance Education.* New York: Oxford University Press.

Reedy, P. 2003. *Body, Mind, and Spirit in Action: A Teacher's Guide to Creative Dance.* Berkeley, CA: Luna Kids Dance.

Reynolds, N. 1979. *The Dance Catalog: A Complete Guide to Today's World of Dance.* New York: Harmony Books.

Shook, K. 1977. *The Elements of Classical Ballet Technique as Practiced in the School of the Dance Theatre of Harlem.* Brooklyn, NY: Dance Horizons.

Solomon, R.; S. C. Minton; and J. Solomon, eds. *Preventing Dance Injuries: An Interdisciplinary Perspective.* 1990. Reston, VA: American Alliance for Health, Physical Education, Recreation and Dance.

Stinson S. W. 1990. "Dance Education in Early Childhood," *Design for Arts in Education,* Vol. 91, No. 6, 34–41.

Stransky, J., and R. B. Stone. 1981. *The Alexander Technique: Joy in the Life of Your Body.* New York: Beaufort Books.

Vaganova, A. 1946. *Basic Principles of Classical Ballet: Russian Ballet Technique.* New York: Kamin Dance Publishers (reprinted in 1969 by Dover Publications, Inc., New York).

Wardle, F. "Folk Dancing for Young Children," *Early Childhood News: The Professional Resource for Teachers and Parents.* http://www.earlychildhoodnews.com/earlychildhood/article_view.aspx?ArticleId=301 (accessed November 1, 2008 and February 23, 2009).

Wright, S. 1985. *Dancer's Guide to Injuries of the Lower Extremity: Diagnosis, Treatment, and Care.* New York: Cornwall Books

FOUNDATIONS IN
Physical Development

Physical development is often thought of as something that happens naturally when children receive adequate nutrition and the opportunity for active physical play. Although some children develop physical skills and concepts with little adult intervention, research on young children's physical development indicates that many children may never fully develop their physical skills without adult encouragement and instruction. Physical development and physical activity play an important role in health throughout a child's life span. In particular, being physically active protects against cardiovascular disease, diabetes, and obesity. It also contributes to mental health and psychological well-being. Physical development, including fundamental movement skills, perceptual–motor skills, and movement concepts, provides the foundation for much of what preschool children do throughout the day. Physical development allows children to engage with others, to explore, to learn, and to play. It is critical to children's overall development and to important public health challenges. Physical development therefore deserves the same level of attention and resources in early childhood programs as other domains of the preschool curriculum.

Fundamental Movement Skills and Movement Concepts

During the preschool years, children develop fundamental movement skills. Those skills are rooted in the perceptual–motor behavior children demonstrate in infancy and toddlerhood. Movement skills are a foundation for learning. They are also a foundation for the more complex motor skills needed later in life for fitness activities, organized sports, and recreation. Young children's fundamental movement skills are progressively elaborated, refined, and consolidated in elementary, middle, and high school. Movement skills, such as running, jumping, or galloping, are broadly defined and described (see the Glossary for definitions). Extensive research indicates that children typically achieve fundamental movement skills in an orderly sequence. The age at which a skill emerges and the rate at which a child achieves these skills varies from child to child (Branta, Haubenstricker, and Seefeldt 1984; Haywood and Getchell 2005).[1]

---

[1] When motor development differs significantly from the expected sequence, it may be appropriate to follow up with a specialist (pediatrician, special education specialist, physical or occupational therapist, or other knowledgeable professional) to determine whether an underlying disability or special need exists.

Preschool children are developmentally primed and highly motivated to learn and become proficient in new movement skills (Sanders 2002). The preschool period is the most opportune time for children to learn fundamental movement skills (Bredekamp and Copple 1997; Gallahue and Cleland-Donnelly 2003; Gallahue and Ozmun 2006a). The rapid physical growth of infancy levels off in early childhood and remains constant until puberty. This plateau allows preschool children to focus on learning how to use their bodies rather than on constantly adapting to their bodies' rapid change in size and weight (van der Meer and van der Weel 1999). The goal for preschool children is to develop reasonable proficiency, not expertise, in a wide variety of movement activities. At this age, children rarely achieve mastery of these skills (Walkley and others 1993). Once proficiency is achieved, those movement skills can be sustained throughout life.

Active Physical Play in the Natural World

When the benefits of preschool are considered, it is important to remember how much children learn through physical activity outdoors in the natural world. Much of the time that children used to spend in outdoor play is now spent in front of a television or computer screen. A recent study of physical activity in preschool programs found that programs with the most screen time (time in front of televisions and computers) had the least amount of active physical play (Dowda and others 2009). A review of the literature on the beneficial effects of nature on children suggests that children prefer spending time in natural settings and that being disconnected from the natural environment negatively affects children's well-being. Research shows that when children, especially those from lower socioeconomic urban communities, have access to green, outdoor spaces, they have better cognitive functioning and improved well-being and social connectedness (Wells and Evans 2003). In those areas of California where outdoor conditions make outdoor physical activity challenging, preschool programs need to find creative ways to preserve children's connection to the natural world, such as structuring the day so that children spend time outside during the early morning before temperatures rise.

Physical development also depends on the environment. Time spent outdoors is a strong determinant of vigorous physical activity in preschool-age children (Baranowski and others 1993; McKenzie and others 2002). Children need space that is adequate in both size and complexity to develop fundamental movement skills and concepts. Children play longer and more vigorously when programs provide play equipment (especially simple, inexpensive, and portable equipment such as balls, tricycles, and hoops), physical activity education, and space for active play (Boldemann and others 2006; Bower and others 2008; Dowda and others 2004, 2009).

The Role of Preschools and Families

Research demonstrates the benefits of a quality preschool experience, particularly for at-risk young children (Cannon and Karoly 2007; Isaacs 2007). Children who do not have safe physical places to play in their home neighborhoods may especially be at a disadvantage in terms of their physical development. For those children, preschool may provide their only opportunity for engaging in active physical play. Some parents may not have the time to supervise children in active outdoor play, provide instruction, or model fundamental movement skills.

Children in California come from diverse cultures. In these diverse cultures, the importance of physical activity to children's socialization and expectations about parental involvement in children's active physical play vary. For example, some children are sent to school in their best clothes and are not encouraged to engage in the rough-and-tumble play that promotes the development of fundamental movement skills. In other families, physical activity is regarded as less important than intellectual activities, such as being read to, learning the sounds of letters, or using a computer. Such family practices may conflict with the goals of preschool educators: to offer all children the opportunity to engage in active physical play and develop proficiency in movement skills. Diverse ways of understanding and approaching active physical play and physical development must be bridged by building relationships between parents and preschool programs. Given opportunity and encouragement, all boys and girls can achieve the skills and knowledge described in the physical development foundations.

The Importance of Movement

Movement provides one way for young children to develop physically, cognitively, and emotionally. Through play and movement, young children move to learn and learn to move (Doherty and Bailey 2003; Gallahue 1982; Rickard and others 1995a). They develop a sense of competence through their movement in relation to the physical and social world, which is not achieved in other ways. This finding may be especially true for children who are English learners, who can enjoy physical activity and become proficient at movement skills while using their home language. Children learn social skills through movement activities. For instance, one study found that children in a Head Start program showed enhanced social competence and behavior after participating in a creative dance and movement intervention (Lobo and Winsler 2006). Studies of elementary school children who exercise consistently show improved cognitive performance (Coe and others 2006; Sallis and others 1999; Trost 2007). Fine motor skills using the hands and fingers (such as cutting with scissors or painting at an easel) help young children to develop the strength and dexterity needed to manipulate a pencil on paper, an important skill for school-readiness.

Time for Active Physical Play

It is often assumed, especially by parents, that young children in preschool are active throughout the day. However, recent studies indicate that young children spend most of the day in sedentary activities and spend less than 5 percent of the day in moderate to vigorous physical activity (Brown and others 2009; Dowda and others 2009; Finn, Johannsen, and Specker 2002; Montgomery and others 2004; Pate and others 2004; Reilly and others 2004). One recent study of private, faith-based, and Head Start programs found that the average preschool child engaged in only about eight minutes of

PHYSICAL DEVELOPMENT

moderate to vigorous activity and two minutes of vigorous physical activity per hour of attendance at preschool (Pate and others 2004). Research also indicates that teacher-designed activities to enhance or encourage children's physical activity are rarely implemented (Brown and others 2009).

Amount of Physical Activity

It is difficult to study fitness in young children. A recent review pointed out that currently there is not enough research on preschool children to identify how much physical activity is necessary for them to maintain a healthy body weight or physical fitness or how much active physical play is needed for adequate development of motor skills (Timmons, Naylor, and Pfeiffer 2007). How much physical activity is needed to prevent children from becoming overweight or obese is not known (Ekelund 2008). However, it is clear that American children of all ages are showing the effects of insufficient activity and poor nutrition.

More than three million children in California (33 percent) are overweight or obese (Children Now 2009). Public health professionals argue that it makes sense to promote the development of exercise habits early in life in order to reduce the risks of adult disease later (Rowland 2007). Even though research cannot say exactly how much physical activity is needed for cardiovascular health or to maintain a healthy weight in preschool children, expectations for physical activity should be established based on best practices. The goal is to ensure that preschool children develop proficiency in movement skills and preserve their health. This goal is especially a worthwhile one for children with chronic health conditions or physical disabilities. Structured physical activities and instruction my have to be adapted in order to develop children's movement skills. In turn, they earn the confidence, social acceptance, and self-esteem that come with being able to perform movement skills.

The recommendations for physical activity that represent current best practice for preschool programs were developed by the National Association for Sport and Physical Education (NASPE). Those standards state that preschoolers should have a cumulative total of at least 60 minutes daily of structured physical activity, at least 60 minutes and up to several hours of unstructured physical activity, and should not be sedentary for more that 60 minutes at a time except when sleeping (NASPE 2002). The recommendations are intended for an entire 24-hour day.

Preschool programs, especially half-day programs, cannot provide children with the total recommended amount physical activity. The Early Childhood Environmental Rating Scale (Harms, Clifford, and Cryer 2005), for instance, has a recommendation that physical activity for children be scheduled daily for both morning and afternoon. This instrument indicates that children in full-day early childhood programs (more than four hours per day) should get one hour a day of gross motor play, and children in half-day programs should get 30 minutes (Harms, Clifford, and Cryer 2005). The accreditation standards of the National Association for the Education of Young Children (2005) recommend that children have the opportunity to play outdoors daily, weather permitting, but do not suggest amounts of physical activity per day.

Physical activity needs to take place in the context of the child's entire day, not just in the early learning environment. However, physical activity can and should be integrated into the preschool curriculum throughout the day. Preschool programs must also partner with families to ensure that children get enough physical activity in the course of the day. This partnership requires ongoing communication with parents about the importance of physical activity. Strategies for integrating physical activity into the preschool day and for working with families to promote physical activity are addressed in the *California Preschool Curriculum Framework, Volume 2* (forthcoming).

Structured physical activity means movement experiences designed by teachers to support learning. In the context of preschool children, it means developmentally appropriate activities that:

- Involve all children and provide frequent participation time.
- Preserve the joy and exuberance that young children bring to physical activity.
- Focus on the process (such as how to kick a ball), not the end result (such as whether the child hits the ball or scores a goal).
- Recognize the wide range of movement skills, fitness, and previous movement experiences of young children and avoid comparison and competition.
- Respond to the needs of individual children for instruction and encouragement.

Physical activity is often thought of as an outdoor activity. Recent research suggests that most vigorous physical activity in preschool programs does take place outdoors (Brown and others 2009). Nevertheless, a program that integrates physical activity into the curriculum throughout the day will take advantage of opportunities for active physical play, both indoors and outdoors. It is especially important for programs that have limited outdoor space or extreme weather conditions to do so.

The Pattern of Movement Skill and Fine Motor Development

Neurological development follows a fixed sequence, starting from the head and moving down to the feet and from the center of the body to the outside (from the trunk to the shoulder to the arms and then hands). Preschool children look less coordinated with their legs and feet than with their arms and hands because of this incomplete *cephalocaudal* (that is, head to toe) development. For instance, four-year-old children tend to run with their feet flat on the ground. As they develop neurologically, their legs and feet become better coordinated. In addition, five-year-old children run more rhythmically on the balls of their feet. Movement skill and concept development unfold through a process in which the child's physical and cultural environment, genetic and physical makeup, and personality and interests all play a role (Newell 1984).

Children develop movement skills and concepts at different rates, especially up to kindergarten. This variability may be especially evident in children with special needs. In the domain of physical development, the suggested age ranges for the achievement of movement skills should be viewed as approximate guides. They represent the developmental path of a majority of children, but individual children often show great variability in the timing of their skill achievements. Differences of as much as a year in the achievement of movement skills are not uncommon in typically developing children (Gallahue and Ozmun 2006a; Payne and Isaacs 2005).

Evidence also suggests that preschool children who participate in high-quality movement education programs may develop movement skills and concepts earlier and more competently than do those children who receive no instruction and little opportunity for practice (Reilly and others 2006). Furthermore, the quality of a child's skill performance may vary depending on the task, the goal, the environment, the equipment, and the level of competition (Lam 2005; Newell 1984; O'Conner 2000). For instance, a child who is just beginning to learn how to throw a ball may perform better in a relaxed rather than a competitive situation, as competition shifts the focus from learning a skill to the end product. Research indicates that children who receive instruction in fundamental motor skills make significant gains in motor-skill acquisition (Connor-Kuntz and Dummer 1996; Goodway and Branta 2003; Reilly and others 2006). Children who have poor-quality movement skills and receive no remediation often avoid what they are not able to do, compounding their challenges.

Preschool children also need experiences that support the development of fine motor skills in their hands and fingers. Children should have strength and dexterity in their hands and fingers before beginning to manipulate a pencil on paper. Working on dexterity and strength first can eliminate the development of an inappropriate pencil grasp, which is becoming more common as young children engage in writing experiences before their hands are ready. Children should also have experiences with equipment that encourages small-muscle skill development, such as puzzles, beads, and string, play dough, and scissors.

Developmentally Appropriate Movement Education

The traditional physical education approach taken in elementary school is not effective for preschool children. Movement programs for young children should reflect their physical maturation and developmental needs and interests. Programs should also adapt to the learning needs of individual children (Gallahue 1995; NASPE 2003). Adaptation to individual learning needs is especially relevant because of the epidemic of childhood obesity in the United States. A child's decision to ride a bicycle or watch television may hinge on his feelings of competence in physical activity or movement skills. These, in turn, depend on developmentally appropriate instruction, opportunities for practice, and adult encouragement and feedback.

The preschool teacher is in a unique position—with experience in observing children's development—to notice when a child fails to make developmental gains in movement abilities. That child may benefit from evaluation and intervention. Teachers need to keep in mind that children can vary as much as year in the timing of their movement skills. On the other hand, there is a need for the teacher's good

judgment in distinguishing between a child whose gross motor lag is explained by his current interest in language learning or simply inexperience with the equipment. A child with a possible neurodevelopmental issue may benefit from intervention. There is ample evidence that children with motor delays benefit from early intervention (Harris 1996; Pakula and Palmer 1996). Intervention can help preschool children who have coordination difficulties or neurodevelopmental delays to improve their movement skills. It may also help prevent compromised physical health and fitness, academic difficulties, and self-esteem problems (Winnick and Lavay 2005).

It is commonly assumed that children will develop essential motor skills naturally and automatically in the course of child-initiated play. Of course, play is extremely important. However, many children require instruction and practice in order to become proficient in movement skills. When opportunities for instruction, practice, and encouragement are provided, children expand and refine their movement skill repertoire. Movement delays may be prevented (Garcia and others 2002). When educators stand aside as observers on the playground, they may inadvertently model inactivity and miss opportunities to provide instruction and to support practice.

Teachers should intentionally engage children in playground activities during some part of the day. Training in movement-skill development and in related instructional strategies is important for preschool teachers. Studies show that movement skills can be improved in young children when they receive quality instruction and practice opportunities, particularly when there is music (Conner-Kuntz and Dummer 1996; Gallahue 2005; Zachopoulou, Tsapakidou, and Derri 2004). Parents also play an important role in helping children develop fundamental motor skills (Miller 1978; Rickard and others 1995a). However, many preschool teachers currently receive little or no training in movement education. This omission needs to be addressed in preservice and inservice teacher education programs. When teachers are prepared to provide the necessary resources, the preschool experience can both preserve and build children's natural enjoyment of physical play. Training can also help teachers understand the importance of physical activity for health.

The Consequences of Inactivity

The dramatic trend toward increased overweight and obesity among all age groups of children and youth, including preschool children, is clearly associated with decreases in physical activity as well as increases in the consumption of high-calorie foods (American Heart Association 2004; American Obesity Association 2002; Dietz 1995; National Center for Education in Maternal and Child Health 2002; Ogden and others 2002; NASPE 2004). Many children start on the path to obesity during the preschool period (Blair and others 2007; Ekelund and others 2006; Nader and others 2006). Risk factors for heart disease are common by age three and tend to continue over time (Williams and others 1998).

The preschool period is an opportune time for young children to learn

fundamental movement skills. Unfortunately, if children do not learn these skills during the preschool period, they may have difficulty learning them later. Their ability to participate in physical activities may be affected later in life, including activities that are important for physical and mental health (McKenzie 2004; Seefeldt 1980). Providing children with opportunities to learn skills is important; as children engage in such learning, teachers need to be sensitive to the fact that some children may have mild to moderate physical disabilities that have not yet been identified.

Physical inactivity is common during early childhood in the United States. Physically inactive children tend to remain more inactive than their peers (Pate and others 1996; Telama and others 1997). Physicality is associated with psychological well-being in children (Parfitt and Eston 2005). Research suggests that athletic ability is a prized attribute among children (Chase and Drummer 1992; Poinsett 1996; Weiss 2004). Children who are athletically competent tend to be more popular with their peers than children with movement difficulties (Rose, Larkin, and Berger 1997; Weiss, Smith, and Theeboom 1996). Children with movement difficulties have been found to be less vigorously active, use play equipment less often, and spend less time interacting with other children (Bouffard and others 1996). Children with poor coordination and movement skills are more often bullied and criticized (Portman 1995), are excluded by others (Evans and Roberts 1987), and have more anxiety and lower self-esteem (Losse and others 1991; Skinner and Piek 2001). They also have lower self-perceptions of physical appearance, athletic competence, and sense of self-worth (Piek, Baynam, and Barrett 2006).

Those issues may be exacerbated in children with physical disabilities whose movement-skill performance may be delayed or different from their typically developing peers (Diamond 1996). Children five to eight years of age with difficulties in motor learning have been shown to have significantly lower physical fitness and a significantly higher body mass index than their peers (Hands and Larkin 2006). These consequences of poor movement skill abilities can be made worse as children repeatedly withdraw from physical activity to avoid embarrassment (Evans and Roberts 1987).

The Preschool Foundations for Physical Development

The preschool learning foundations for physical development are organized in terms of three broad categories or strands:

- Fundamental Movement Skills
- Perceptual–Motor Skills and Movement Concepts
- Active Physical Play

The first strand, Fundamental Movement Skills, includes the substrands of Balance, Locomotor Skills, and Manipulative Skills. The second strand, Perceptual–Motor Skills and Movement Concepts, includes the substrands of Body Awareness, Spatial Awareness, and Directional Awareness. The third strand, Active Physical Play, comprises the substrands of Active Participation; Cardiovascular Endurance; and Muscular Strength, Muscular Endurance, and Flexibility.

Within each substrand, the foundations describe the knowledge and skills most children demonstrate at around 48 and 60 months of age. Although the foundations describe knowledge and skills at around 48 and 60 months of age, it is important to understand that the foundations are age-related and not age-dependent. The foundations are illustrated by examples that put the behavior in context. Examples show the foundation as seen through the behavior of a particular child or children. When examples are given that indicate verbal expression, the child may use any language, including American Sign Language. For more information about children's second-language development, please see the *California Preschool Learning Foundations, Volume 1*, in English Language Development.

Bibliographic notes are provided later and offer further information and references to the research. How to support the development of children's knowledge, skills, and behaviors related to physical development is addressed in the *California Preschool Curriculum Framework, Volume 2* (forthcoming).

Overview of the Foundations

Fundamental Movement Skills

1.0 Balance
   1.1, 1.2
2.0 Locomotor Skills
   2.1, 2.2, 2.3, 2.4
3.0 Manipulative Skills
   3.1, 3.2

Perceptual–Motor Skills and Movement Concepts

1.0 Body Awareness
   1.1
2.0 Spatial Awareness
   2.1
3.0 Directional Awareness
   3.1, 3.2, 3.3, 3.4

Active Physical Play

1.0 Active Participation
   1.1
2.0 Cardiovascular Endurance
   2.1
3.0 Muscular Strength, Muscular Endurance, and Flexibility
   3.1

Fundamental Movement Skills

1.0 Balance

PHYSICAL DEVELOPMENT

At around 48 months of age	*At around 60 months of age*
1.1 Maintain balance while holding still; sometimes may need assistance.	**1.1** Show increasing balance and control when holding still.
Examples	**Examples**
• Pretends to be a flamingo by standing balanced on one foot, with or without assistance, for several seconds using arms to balance. • Stands still with eyes open; arms may swing side to side to maintain balance. • Able to "freeze" after running; arms may swing side to side to maintain balance. • Able to stand still while holding onto a shopping cart or walker.*	• Pretends to be a flamingo by standing on one foot, unassisted, for five or more seconds without touching a nearby object, such as a wall or a table, for support. • Balances on three body parts (for example, two hands and one foot). • Stands still while holding arms at side when the song says, "Freeze!" • Balances a beanbag on top of head for several seconds.
1.2 Maintain balance while in motion when moving from one position to another or when changing directions, though balance may not be completely stable.	**1.2** Show increasing balance control while moving in different directions and when transitioning from one movement or position to another.
Examples	**Examples**
• Walks forward on a wide line (or tape) on the floor, alternating feet with or without assistance. • Sways back and forth moving a scarf higher and higher in the air, reaching out to the arm of wheelchair with other hand to catch body as the arc of the movement increases. • While walking on the sandbox border, is able to maintain balance for several steps, wobbles, rights self, and continues. • Swings hips, with feet together, when playing with a hula hoop. • During the song "Head, Shoulders, Knees, and Toes," maintains balance while reaching for toes.	• Walks forward and backward on a wide line (or tape) on the floor without assistance. • Able to step from circle to circle by using a walker. • Walks on the edge of the sandbox area. • Completes a sequence of dynamic and static balances, as in the game Statues or while playing Simon Says. • Runs up an incline, avoiding a playmate stopped midway.

Note: Many examples in this section describe movement skills that may look different in children with physical disabilities. When possible, early educators should check with family and specialists regarding the child's movement skill development.
*Walker: When used in examples, it indicates a therapeutic walker specifically prescribed for a child in need of support when walking.

2.0 Locomotor Skills

At around 48 months of age	At around 60 months of age
2.1 Walk with balance, not always stable, oppositional arm movements still developing, and relatively wide base of support (space between feet).	**2.1** Walk with balance, oppositional arm movements, and relatively narrow base of support (space between feet).
Examples	**Examples**
• Walks up stairs, using alternating feet, without support. • Child with leg braces walks down stairs with support from wall or handrail. • Attempts to follow lines or simple patterns on the floor. • Pretends to be a tightrope walker in a balancing act in the circus, waving arms to maintain balance.	• Walks down steps, alternating feet, without support. • Follows more complicated patterns on the floor; for example, a zigzag pattern in the carpet. • Follows a line or simple pattern on the floor, using slow and then fast walking movements when prompted. • Balances beanbags on different parts of the body while walking along pathways taped in straight and circular lines.
2.2 Run with short stride length and feet off the ground for a short period of time. May show inconsistent opposition of arms and legs.	**2.2** Run with a longer stride length and each foot off the ground for a greater length of time. Opposition of arms and legs is more consistent.
Examples	**Examples**
• Runs unevenly; one arm may pump more. • Runs but has difficulty stopping with control; for example, while playing tag, runs and has difficulty stopping at the intended location. • Runs with feet flat on the ground.	• Runs evenly, arms pumping in opposition. • Runs and stops with control; for example, while playing tag, stops at intended location. • Runs lightly on toes. • Zigzags when running in the yard to avoid structures and playmates.
2.3 Jump for height (up or down) and for distance with beginning competence.	**2.3** Jump for height (up or down) and for distance with increasing competence. Uses arm swing to aid forward jump.
Examples	**Examples**
• Tries to jump up and bump a hanging object, such as a beach or foam ball suspended from a low ceiling. • Jumps forward a couple of feet using a two-footed takeoff and landing. • Jumps like a frog (squatting, with hands on ground) from one "lily pad" to another (close distances). • Jumps off a curb or low playground equipment, landing on two feet.	• Jumps over a block by using a two-footed takeoff with arm swing. • Jumps forward a distance of about three feet. • Jumps over the rope as an adult in the middle of a circle slowly swings a rope with a beanbag tied to the end close to the ground in a circle. Children around the circle jump to avoid the beanbag swinging under their feet.

2.0 Locomotor Skills *(Continued)*

At around 48 months of age	*At around 60 months of age*
2.4 Begin to demonstrate a variety of locomotor skills, such as galloping, sliding, hopping, and leaping.	**2.4** Demonstrate increasing ability and body coordination in a variety of locomotor skills, such as galloping, sliding, hopping, and leaping.
Examples	**Examples**
<ul><li>Pretends to be a horse, galloping rapidly but with some body stiffness.</li><li>Makes sliding movements, usually not smoothly; may have trailing foot going past lead foot, looking uncoordinated.</li><li>Hops forward on one foot once or twice, with the nonsupporting leg in front of the body.</li><li>Runs and steps over a rope or beanbag on the floor; action looks like an exaggerated run rather than a true leap over an object.</li></ul>	<ul><li>Pretends to be a horse, galloping with rhythmic pattern and relaxed.</li><li>Slides smoothly and rhythmically.</li><li>Hops a distance of several feet, landing on preferred foot.</li><li>Hops in and out of hoops, with the nonsupporting leg hanging down or behind the supporting leg.</li><li>Leaps over a "river" made from two ropes by starting with a run, taking off with one foot, and landing on the other foot.</li></ul>

3.0 Manipulative Skills

At around 48 months of age	At around 60 months of age
3.1 Begin to show gross motor manipulative skills by using arms, hands, and feet, such as rolling a ball underhand, tossing underhand, bouncing, catching, striking, throwing overhand, and kicking.	**3.1** Show gross motor manipulative skills by using arms, hands, and feet with increased coordination, such as rolling a ball underhand, tossing underhand, bouncing, catching, striking, throwing overhand, and kicking.
Examples	**Examples**
• Tries to roll a ball the size of a tennis ball by bending over and tossing rather than rolling, stepping forward with foot on same side as throwing arm. • Begins to toss a ball underhand, using one or both hands. • Uses an underhand toss to try to hit a target from several feet away. • Bounces a ball more than once to catch from a stationary position; palm of hand may be flat with a loose wrist. • Catches a ball or object by trapping it against the body with arms. • Takes two or three tries to catch a large playground ball from about five feet away using both hands. • Strikes a beach ball off the table with hands, sometimes losing balance. • Takes a step when throwing beanbags, tennis balls, yarn balls, or rubber balls overhand to big targets from about five to ten feet away. • Kicks a stationary ball with back swing that starts at the knee, leaning slightly forward, with little follow-through of leg and limited arm action.	• Rolls a ball underhand, stepping forward on opposite foot and releasing the ball using one hand. • Toss an object underhand into a basket from about six feet away. • Catches a ball or object with hands, absorbing the force of the throw with the body. • Bounces a ball once, then catches it with two hands. • With arms bent and using only hands, catches a small ball thrown from about five feet away. • Strikes a stationary or moving object smoothly and with control, with a soft bat, stepping toward the object. • Throws a ball overhand forcefully with full arm swing, leaning forward and stepping forward with the leg opposite the throwing arm. • Kicks with full leg swing, arms moving in opposition to the legs.

3.0 Manipulative Skills *(Continued)*

At around 48 months of age	*At around 60 months of age*
3.2 Begin to show fine motor manipulative skills using hands and arms such as in-hand manipulation, writing, cutting, and dressing.	**3.2** Show increasing fine motor manipulative skills using hands and arms such as in-hand manipulation, writing, cutting, and dressing.
Examples	**Examples**
• Grasps marker between thumb and pad of index finger, with marker resting on the first joint of the middle finger. • Duplicates simple large shapes, such as a circle and a cross. • Paints with intentional direction at easel or places color in certain places on the paper. • Cuts out a small paper circle, making gradual changes in the direction of cutting. • "Melts monsters" by using a spray bottle to squirt at a picture of a monster drawn with a marker. • Buttons and unbuttons one button on a shirt while playing in the dramatic play area. • Puts socks on correctly with heel in place.	• Makes slight adjustments of tools in the hand while writing or cutting. • Duplicates shapes, such as a square and a triangle. • Repositions a paintbrush to keep the paint from dripping while painting at an easel. • Cuts out a small paper square, making precise changes in the direction of cutting. • Threads a belt through a belt loop on pants. • Puts on jacket, latches zipper, and zips it.

PHYSICAL DEVELOPMENT

Perceptual–Motor Skills and Movement Concepts

1.0 Body Awareness

At around 48 months of age	At around 60 months of age
1.1 Demonstrate knowledge of the names of body parts.	**1.1** Demonstrate knowledge of an increasing number of body parts.
Examples	**Examples**
• Follows directions that include body part name; for example, "Put the smock over your head." • Points to, touches, or indicates a variety of body parts such as head, arm, knee, heel, elbow, and chin correctly while participating in a body-part action song (such as the "Hokey Pokey" or "Head, Shoulders, Knees, and Toes"). • Communicates, "Don't forget my fingertips!" while creating a body tracing.	• While drawing, names and adds body parts. • While assembling a puzzle, points to, touches, or indicates an increasing number of body parts; for example, waist, wrist, ankle, hip, and shoulder. • Indicates which body part is injured: "I hit my elbow on the slide."

Note: In this section, keep in mind that a child with physical disabilities may understand many of the movement concepts without being able to demonstrate them. Additionally, children with significant visual impairments or those who are blind will demonstrate delays in some motor areas directly due to their disability. For more information, see the Bibliographic Notes.

2.0 Spatial Awareness

At around 48 months of age	*At around 60 months of age*
2.1 Use own body as reference point when locating or relating to other people or objects in space.	**2.1** Use own body, general space, and other people's space when locating or relating to other people or objects in space.

Examples	Examples
• Says, "My ball is too far away to reach," or "That branch is too high up to get." • Maintains space, with guidance and assistance, around self without touching or bumping into others during activities. • Reacts late sometimes to a person or an obstacle in the path. • Demonstrates over/under, on/off, in/out, above/below, through/around, and next to with a hula hoop. • Demonstrates awareness of the need to maintain personal space between himself and others when climbing a ladder with other children on the playground.	• Tries to throw a ball to a friend. Says, "Get closer! No, too close. Further back!" • Maintains space around self, in general, during movement activities but sometimes needs to be reminded. • Navigates a human obstacle course, avoiding collisions with other people. • Uses hula hoop and communicates to others, "Watch out; you might get hurt." • Quickly follows teacher's direction to place an object over/under, on/off, in/out, above/below, through/around, next to, near/far, in front/behind, or along/through another object.

3.0 Directional Awareness

At around 48 months of age	At around 60 months of age
3.1 Distinguish movements that are up and down and to the side of the body (for example, understands "use that side, now the other side").	**3.1** Begin to understand and distinguish between the sides of the body.

Examples

- A blind child uses a cane and handrails to negotiate steps to classroom door.
- Attempts to hop on one foot, then the other.
- When a teacher demonstrates looking at the person sitting next to someone on one side and then the other, the child looks right and then left in same sequence.

Examples

- Puts one hand in during the "Hokey Pokey" and then puts the other hand in (not necessarily the "right" and "left" accurately).
- When asked which knee got hurt, can reach across the body to show the correct knee.
- In quick succession, can put beanbag on foot and balance, then on opposite hand stretched out to the side and balance, and then can pass the beanbag around the body.

3.2 Move forward and backward or up and down easily.	**3.2** Can change directions quickly and accurately.

Examples

- Climbs up and down the ladder of a large outdoor play structure.
- Moves forward and backward through a tunnel or a box during play.
- Communicates, "I'm backing up" while sitting on a wheel toy and using her feet to move it.
- Imitates peers moving forward and backward while playing Follow the Leader.

Examples

- Moves forward, backward, up, and down quickly with ease and accuracy through an obstacle course game.
- A child who is nonambulatory uses a wheelchair to travel along a zigzag pattern taped to the floor.
- Plays game of tag by running away from and dodging child who is It.
- Stops and goes quickly when directed while playing Red Light, Green Light.

3.0 Directional Awareness (Continued)

At around 48 months of age	At around 60 months of age
3.3 Can place an object on top of or under something with some accuracy.	**3.3** Can place an object or own body in front of, to the side, or behind something else with greater accuracy.
Examples	**Examples**
• Places special picture brought for sharing on top of cubby, when asked. • Follows directions to put a puzzle away on the shelf under the crayons. • Uses large wood blocks to build a tall tower and says, "Pagoda!"* • Can place hand on top of head during a game of Simon Says.	• Comments to a friend completing a puzzle, "That piece goes in the corner" or "That piece goes next to the dog." • Plays with a farm animal set. Lines the animals standing up in front of the barn door. • Places an item near, far, over, under, between, and through another item when prompted to do so. • Places self in relation to objects in space when following the words of a song; for instance, knowing where to position herself when singing "London Bridge Is Falling Down."
3.4 Use any two body parts together.	**3.4** Demonstrate more precision and efficiency during two-handed fine motor activities.
Examples	**Examples**
• Strings big beads using one hand to hold the string and the other to put beads on. • Cuts shapes by cutting with scissors with one hand and holding paper with the other hand. • Holds popsicle stick with one hand and places glue on stick with other hand. • Can touch hand to opposite knee while marching.	• Strings smaller beads by using one hand to hold the string and the other to put beads on with increasing ease and speed. • Cuts shapes by cutting with scissors with one hand and repositioning paper with the other hand. • When rice is served for lunch (or using own rice from home), holds the rice bowl in one hand and picks up the chopsticks in the other hand to eat the rice. • Hammers a nail into a piece of wood while outdoors and says, "I'm building *mi casa* (my house)."

*A *pagoda* is the general term in English for a tiered tower with multiple eaves. It is common in China, Japan, Korea, Vietnam, and other parts of Asia. Some Asian families have miniature pagodas displayed as decorations at home or have paintings featuring pagodas.

Active Physical Play

1.0 Active Participation

At around 48 months of age	At around 60 months of age
1.1 Initiate or engage in simple physical activities for a short to moderate period of time.	**1.1** Initiate more complex physical activities for a sustained period of time.
Examples	**Examples**
• Rides a tricycle on playground for a period of time alone or with another child who is also riding a tricycle. • Asks child in wheelchair, "Want to go for a walk? I can push you," and pushes child around the playground. • During outside play, engages a friend to race to the fence and back. • Communicates to another child, "Wanna swing on the swings with me?"	• Rides a tricycle for an extended period of time alone or in a made-up game with another child who is also riding a tricycle. • Sits on and bounces a "bouncy ball." • Kicks a soccer ball and runs with a group of other children. • Rolls a hula hoop or a ball and runs beside it with a friend or alone.

PHYSICAL DEVELOPMENT

2.0 Cardiovascular Endurance

At around 48 months of age	At around 60 months of age
2.1 Engage in frequent bursts of active play that involves the heart, the lungs, and the vascular system.	**2.1** Engage in sustained active play of increasing intensity that involves the heart, the lungs, and the vascular system.
Examples	**Examples**
• Engages in a variety of moderate to vigorous activities that raise the heart rate, such as dancing to fast-paced music, playing tag, or running races. • Scoops and gathers dried leaves on a nature walk, then runs to the grass, and throws them in the air or makes a pile and jumps into them. • Engages in frequent bursts of active play inside or outside, followed by periods of rest.	• Engages in a variety of moderate to vigorous activities that raise the heart rate and are more complex, such as jumping into and out of hula hoops, flying kites, or running through an obstacle course. • Maintains active play while playing inside or outside for a longer period of time without tiring. • Gallops rapidly next to a "river" made of ropes and, when prompted, leaps over the river and back again several times.

3.0 Muscular Strength, Muscular Endurance, and Flexibility

At around 48 months of age	*At around 60 months of age*
3.1 Engage in active play activities that enhance leg and arm strength, muscular endurance, and flexibility.	**3.1** Engage in increasing amounts of active play activities that enhance leg and arm strength, muscular endurance, and flexibility.
Examples	**Examples**
• Using an adaptive tricycle, uses legs or arms to maneuver along bike path. • Pulls in a wagon a child who does not walk. • Bends, stretches, twists, and turns, with or without music, through a limited range, sometimes losing balance.	• Child in wheelchair uses arms during parachute play. • Hangs upside down on a bar, holding on with hands and legs. • Pushes and pulls boxes. • Moves through an obstacle course with a variety of increasingly challenging activities that require climbing, jumping, rolling under obstacles, running, and moving on hands and feet. • Bends, stretches, twists, and turns without losing balance and in big movements as part of a dance or game.

Bibliographic Notes

Fundamental Movement Skills

Fundamental movement skills include balance, locomotor skills, and manipulative skills. The term *locomotor skills* describes projecting the body into or through space (for example, running, jumping, hopping, galloping, or skipping). The term *manipulative skills* refers to handling objects by giving to and receiving force from those objects (for example, the gross motor activities of throwing, kicking [van Sleuwen and others 2007]), or catching an object. Manipulative skills also include fine motor activities such as buttoning a button or writing. Balance, along with coordination, is critical for the mastery of fundamental motor skills in the preschool period (Gallahue and Ozmun 2006a). *Dynamic balance* means maintaining balance as the child's center of gravity shifts, for example, while walking on a balance beam. *Static balance* means maintaining balance while the child's center of gravity remains stationary; for instance, balance on one foot without touching anything with any other part of the body to maintain balance. Static balance is substantially related to school-readiness and reading achievement in elementary-age children (Kohen-Raz 1970). Static postures are another component of stability or balance activities and involve bending, stretching, twisting, and turning.

Perceptual–Motor Skills and Movement Concepts

Perceptual–motor coordination is the child's ability to respond physically to incoming sensory information (for example, visual, auditory, touch, and kinesthetic). Coordinated behavior in young children is the ability to quickly and accurately perform certain movements and should be synchronous, rhythmic, and properly sequenced (Garcia 2002). All voluntary movement requires an element of perception. Preschool children's visual perception is not yet mature. They make frequent errors in judgment when assessing distances relative to themselves. Visual acuity and the ability to distinguish an object from its surroundings are improving rapidly but will not be fully mature until around ten years of age. Young children develop perceptual–motor understanding in the following areas: body awareness, spatial awareness, directional awareness, and temporal awareness or rhythmic skills.[2]

Body awareness refers to the ability to accurately describe body parts and their functions. *Laterality* is the ability to distinguish the two sides of the body, which leads to the ability to coordinate the two sides of the body (bilateral coordination). *Spatial awareness* refers to being aware of how much space the body takes up, its relationships to other objects or

---

[2]Temporal awareness is addressed in the dance section of the Visual and Performing Arts foundations.

people in the environment, and being able to project the body into space in different directions (directionality). *Temporal awareness* involves the relationship between movement and time, as in being able to move rhythmically or being able to judge when a ball will reach a hand, or to judge when to turn, when running, to avoid another child or an object on the path.

Perceptual–motor skills are required for coordinated movement and also form the basis for essential concepts associated with success in learning how to read, write, spell, draw, and count. They play an important role in school-readiness. For instance, children who are taught how to write before they develop the necessary sensorimotor skills may become discouraged and develop poor writing practices that are difficult to remediate later (Amundson 2005).

Physical activities in the preschool setting that emphasize perceptual–motor abilities are different from those that emphasize gross motor abilities, and curricula need to include both. There are relationships between fine motor and hand–eye coordination in kindergarten and early school achievement in mathematics and language (Son and Meisel 2006). Children who fail to establish good perceptual–motor skills in preschool will not only have trouble with movement and coordination but may also be at risk of academic failure.

Movement concepts provide understanding about the how, where, with whom, or with what a movement will be performed (Gallahue and Cleland-Donnelly 2003; Ignico 1994). There are three categories or substrands: space, effort, and relationships. *Space* refers to where the body moves. Spatial concepts can be defined by direction (forward, backward, sideways), by level (high, middle or low), or pathways taken (straight, curved, zigzag). *Effort* refers to how the body moves (fast/slow, suddenly/persistently, with strong or light force). *Relationships* refers to the people or things with whom the body moves. Relationships may be with people (together/apart, alone/in a group, following/leading) or with objects (over/under, in/out, above/below, through/around).

A child with physical disabilities may well understand many movement concepts without being able to demonstrate them. Additionally, children with significant visual impairments or those who are blind will demonstrate delays in some motor areas directly due to their disability. For example, a child who is blind will not jump off the ground without holding onto something. Although the child may show delays in motor development, it does not necessarily indicate delays in cognitive development. This point is important because if a teacher expects this level of understanding, she may misjudge the cognitive abilities of a child who cannot see or physically move because the child cannot consistently and broadly show his or her understanding.

Active Physical Play

Children are naturally drawn to, and take pleasure in, active physical play. Play is an essential part of early childhood development. There is evidence that children currently play less in general, play less without adult supervision, and play less outdoors than they did previously (Burdette

and Whitaker 2005; Ginsburg 2007). Active physical play affords children opportunities for problem solving and social interaction; in older children, active physical play has been shown to improve mood and emotional well-being. Although active physical play is promoted as a way to improve children's physical health, it also allows children to experience the joys of movement, creativity, and friendship (Burdette and Whitaker 2005). Those qualities, not a desire to preserve health, draw children to play. Although physical health is an important goal for children, it is best served by preserving children's pleasure in active physical play. Preschool children's play follows a different pattern from that of older children. Young children play vigorously for brief periods in a variety of activities with frequent rest periods (Bailey and others 1995).

Physical fitness is the capacity to perform physical activity and includes the health-related components of aerobic endurance, muscular strength and endurance, joint flexibility, and body composition. It also includes the performance-related components of balance, speed, agility, power, and coordination (Gallahue and Ozmun 2006b). The strand of Active Physical Play addresses the health-related components of physical fitness. Physical fitness is considered one of the most important indicators of physical health, and lack of it plays an important role in the development of cardiovascular disease (Ortega and others 2008).

Aerobic endurance is the ability of the heart, lungs, and vascular system to supply oxygen-rich blood to the body's working muscles during physical activity. Aerobic endurance is considered by most experts to be the most important aspect of physical fitness. Increasing the amount of a child's vigorous physical activity as a way to improve aerobic endurance is advocated by many, though research on fitness in children younger than six is limited (Gallahue and Ozmun 2006b; Rowland 2007). Research is also limited on the aerobic capacity and endurance of preschool children or the amount of physical activity that they need for fitness (Gallahue and Cleland-Donnelly 2003; Timmons, Naylor, and Pfeiffer 2007).

Muscular strength is the maximum amount of work a muscle can do at a given time. Strength naturally increases with age because of body growth and the development of the neuromuscular system (Ortega and others 2008). Muscular endurance is the ability to sustain a physical task, such as climbing stairs repeatedly. There are large increases in strength and endurance between the ages of four and seven.

Glossary

balance. The ability to maintain body control while moving and while still.

base of support. That part of the body that makes contact with the support surface, for instance two feet on the floor, two hands and two feet on the floor, or the pelvis and the lower extremities on the floor when sitting with the legs straight in front.

bilateral coordination. The coordinated use of both hands/arms/sides of the body at the same time.

body awareness. Knowledge about the body and its parts.

body mass index. A number calculated from a person's weight and height. BMI provides a reliable indicator of body fatness for most people and is used to determine a person's weight category. Depending on the category, some BMIs may lead to health problems.

bouncing. A large motor skill that involves giving force to an object with one or both hands and receiving its force back with one or both hands.

cardiovascular endurance. Capacity for sustained, active play. Taking part in activities that involves the heart, the lungs, and the vascular system.

catching. A large motor skill that involves the use of hands to stop and trap a tossed or flying object.

cephalocaudal. From the head to tail. Refers to neurological development that proceeds from the head down to the feet.

directional awareness. Where the body moves. Includes handedness, laterality, sequence, and rhythm.

directionality. The ability to project the body's spatial dimensions into surrounding space and to grasp spatial concepts about the movements or locations of objects in the environment.

dynamic balance. Maintaining balance while in motion.

fine motor activity. A physical activity, such as using crayons, stacking blocks, or cutting with scissors, that uses the smaller muscle groups of primarily the fingers, hands, and wrists.

flexibility. Range of motion of a joint and the elasticity of muscle and connective tissues.

flight phase. The short period of the stride, typically when running, where both feet are off the ground.

fundamental movement skills. Observable patterns of motor behavior that requires the coordination of different body parts. Fundamental movement patterns are classified into three categories: locomotor skills such as running and jumping; manipulative or object-control skills such as throwing and catching; and balance skills such as standing on one foot or walking on a narrow beam. Fundamental movement skills are the building blocks for more complex future movements.

galloping. Making a forward step motion with a leading foot followed by a leap motion of the trailing foot.

gross motor activity. A physical activity, such as throwing, striking, running, or jumping, that uses the major muscle groups of the arms, legs, and trunk.

hopping. Projecting the body in space by taking off on one foot and landing on the same foot. Hopping is a more complicated version of jumping and requires a higher degree of strength and finer adjustments in balance.

in-hand manipulation. A small-muscle skill that involves adjusting an object in the hand after it is grasped.

intensity. Engaging in physical activity that involves maximal effort.

PHYSICAL DEVELOPMENT

jumping. Projecting of the body into the air from a force generated by arms and one or two feet and landing on two feet. There are three forms of jumping: jumping (up) for height, jumping for distance, jumping (down) from a distance. Jumping requires coordination of all body parts.

kicking. A large motor skill that is a form of striking in which one foot is used to apply force to the ball.

kinesthetic. Of or relating to movement.

kinesthetic sense. Awareness of the position and movement of one's body parts during physical activities.

laterality. The awareness that one's body has two separate sides that can move independently. The most obvious example of laterality is handedness, or the preference for using one hand over the other to perform activities. Preschool children cannot yet identify right and left, but they can distinguish one side of their bodies from the other and coordinate movements of the two sides (bilateral coordination). For example, they can hold a beach ball in one hand and hit it with the other hand. Laterality must develop before children can develop directionality.

leaping. Running and then taking off with one foot with an elongated step and landing on the opposite foot. It looks like a big step with an extended flight phase in the air.

locomotor skills. The ability to project the body into or through space.

manipulative skills. Also known as object-control skills in which the arms, hands, legs, and feet are used to give force to an object (for example, throwing a ball) or to receive and absorb the force from an object (for example, catching a ball).

motor. Refers to neural "internal" processes operating at a cortical or subcortical level in the brain and is applied to motor development, motor learning, motor control, and motor behavior (Gallahue and Ozmun 2006a, Chapter 1).

movement. The "external" manifestation of internal motor processes and is used in the terms *movement education* and *movement skills* (Gallahue and Ozmun 2006a, Chapter 1).

movement skills. Observable, goal-directed movement patterns.

muscular endurance. The ability to exert force against an object external to the body for several repetitions without tiring.

muscular strength. The amount of force the muscle can produce. Strong-effort activities involving different muscle groups or the whole body are key factors in muscular strength.

nonambulatory. Inability to walk independently.

obesity. Overweight and obesity are both labels for ranges of weight that are greater than what is generally considered healthy for a given height. A child who has a BMI-for-age that falls at the 95th percentile or higher is considered obese. An adult who has a BMI of 30 or higher is considered obese. BMI for children is age- and gender-specific and is best determined by using a BMI calculator.

overweight. A child with a BMI-for-age that falls between the 85th to less than the 95th percentile is considered overweight. An adult who has a BMI between 25 and 29.9 is considered overweight.

physical activity. Any body movement produced by skeletal muscles that results in the expenditure of energy.

physical fitness. A set of attributes that people have or achieve that relates to the ability to perform physical activity, including characteristics such as cardiorespiratory endurance, muscular strength and endurance, body composition, flexibility, and balance. Physical fitness is mainly determined by physical activity patterns over recent weeks and months.

physicality. The quality of being full of energy and force; the quality or condition of being physical.

relationships. The relationship of the body to its parts, people, objects, and the combinations of all these elements.

rolling ball underhand. A large muscle skill that involves projecting a ball on the floor. To roll the ball underhand, the child bends knees, steps with opposite foot, swings the arm back, and then swings the arm forward to release the ball close to the ground; the arm follows through toward the target.

running. Projecting of the body into space with an alternative foot support, such as walking, and a flight phase when both feet are off the ground.

sliding. Demonstrating a form of galloping in which the child steps purposefully in a sideward direction.

spatial awareness. How a child moves her body in space and awareness of how much space the body takes up; its relationship to other objects or people in the environment; and ability to project the body into space.

static balance. Maintaining balance while still.

striking. A large motor skill that involves the action of giving force to an object by propelling it in the air with a hand or an implement, such as a paddle, racket, or bat.

temporal awareness. Sequence, synchronicity, and rhythm when one moves in space.

throwing overhand. A large motor skill that involves projecting a ball in a forward direction using an overarm action and stepping in opposition. The ball is released in front of the body (like a baseball throw).

tossing underhand. A large motor skill that involves projecting an object in a forward direction by using an underarm action and stepping with the opposite foot; object is released at waist level.

vascular system. The heart and the blood vessels (arteries, veins, and capillaries) that distribute blood to the body.

walker. When used in examples, indicates a therapeutic walker specifically prescribed for a child as support for walking.

walking. Transferring weight from one foot to another while moving across the floor.

References and Source Materials

Alpert, B., and others. 1990. "Aerobics Enhances Cardiovascular Fitness and Agility in Preschoolers," *Health Psychology*, Vol. 9, No. 1, 48–56.

American Heart Association. 2004. *Exercise (Physical Activity) and Children*. http://www.americanheart.org/presenter.jhtml?identifier=4596 (accessed July 16, 2008).

American Obesity Association. 2002. *Childhood Obesity*. http://obesity.tempdomainname.com/subs/childhood/ (accessed July 16, 2008).

Amundson, S. 2005. "Prewriting and Handwriting Skills," in *Occupational Therapy for Children* (Fifth edition), 587–614. Edited by J. Case-Smith. St. Louis: Elsevier Mosby.

Apache, R. R. 2005. "Activity-Based Intervention in Motor Skill Development," *Perceptual and Motor Skills*, Vol. 100, No. 3, Part 2, 1011–20.

Bailey, R. C., and others. 1995. "The Level and Tempo of Children's Physical Activities: An Observational Study," *Medicine and Science in Sports and Exercise*, Vol. 27, No. 7, 1033–41.

Baranowski, T., and others. 1993. "Observations on Physical Activity in Physical Locations: Age, Gender, Ethnicity, and Month Effects," *Research Quarterly for Exercise and Sport*, Vol. 64, No. 2, 127–33.

Blair, N. J., and others. 2007. "Risk Factors for Obesity in 7-year-old European Children: The Auckland Birthweight Collaborative Study," *Archives of Disease in Childhood*, Vol. 92, No. 10, 866–71.

Boldemann, C., and others. 2006. "Impact of Preschool Environment Upon Children's Physical Activity and Sun Exposure," *Preventive Medicine*, Vol. 42, No. 4, 301–8.

Bouffard, M., and others. 1996. "A Test of the Activity Deficit Hypothesis with Children with Movement Difficulties," *Adapted Physical Activity Quarterly*, Vol. 13, No. 1, 61–73.

Bower, J. K., and others. 2008. "The Childcare Environment and Children's Physical Activity," *American Journal of Preventive Medicine*, Vol. 34, No. 1, 23–29.

Branta, C.; J. Haubenstricker; and V. Seefeldt. 1984. "Age Changes in Motor Skills During Childhood and Adolescence," *Exercise and Sport Sciences Reviews*, Vol. 12, No. 1, 467–520.

Bredekamp, S., and C. Copple, eds. 1997. *Developmentally Appropriate Practice in Early Childhood Programs* (Revised edition). Washington, DC: National Association for the Education of Young Children.

Brown, T.; S. Kelly; and C. Summerbell. "2007. Prevention of Obesity: A Review of Interventions," *Obesity Reviews*, Vol. 8, Supplement 1, 127–30.

Brown, W. H., and others. 2009. "Social and Environmental Factors Associated With Preschoolers' Nonsedentary Physical Activity," *Child Development*, Vol. 80, No. 1, 45–58.

Burdette, H. L., and R. C. Whitaker. 2005. "Resurrecting Free Play in Young Children: Looking Beyond Fitness and Fatness to Attention, Affiliation, and Affect," *Archives of Pediatric and Adolescent Medicine*, Vol. 159, No. 1, 46–50.

Cannon, J. S., and L. A. Karoly. 2007. *Who Is Ahead and Who Is Behind? Gaps in School Readiness and Student Achievement in the Early Grades for California's Children* (No. TR-537PF/WKKF/PEW/NIEER/WCJVSF/LAUP). Santa Monica, CA: Rand Corporation.

Chase, M. A., and G. M. Drummer. 1992. "The Role of Sports as a Social Status Determinant in Children," *Research Quarterly for Exercise and Sport*, Vol. 63, 418–24.

Children Now. 2009. *California Report Card '09: Setting the Agenda for Children.* Oakland, CA: Children Now.

Cleland, F. E., and D. L. Gallahue. 1993. "Young Children's Divergent Movement Ability: Study I," *Perceptual and Motor Skills*, Vol. 77, 535–44.

Coe, D. P., and others. 2006. "Effect of Physical Education and Activity Levels on Academic Achievement in Children," *Medicine and Science in Sports and Exercise*, Vol. 38, No. 8, 1515–19.

Connor-Kuntz, F. J., and G. M. Dummer. 1996. "Teaching Across the Curriculum: Language-Enriched Physical Education for Preschool Children," *Adapted Physical Activity Quarterly*, Vol. 13, No. 3, 302–15.

Diamond, K. E. 1996. "Preschool Children's Conceptions of Disabilities: The Salience of Disability in Children's Ideas About Others," *Topics in Early Childhood Special Education*, Vol. 16, No. 4, 458–75.

Dietz, W. H. 1995. "Childhood Obesity," in *Childhood Health, Nutrition, and Physical Activity*, 155–66. Edited by L. W. Y. Cheung and J. B. Richmond. Champaign, IL: Human Kinetics.

Doherty, J., and R. Bailey. 2003. *Supporting Physical Development and Physical Education in the Early Years.* Philadelphia, PA: Open University Press.

Dowda, M., and others. 2004. "Influences of Preschool Policies and Practices on Children's Physical Activity," *Journal of Community Health*, Vol. 29, No. 3, 183–96.

Dowda, M., and others. 2009. "Policies and Characteristics of the Preschool Environment and Physical Activity of Young Children," *Pediatrics*, Vol. 123, No. 2, 261–66.

Ekelund, U. 2008. "Cardiorespiratory Fitness, Exercise Capacity and Physical Activity in Children: Are We Measuring the Right Thing?" *Archives of Disease in Childhood*, Vol. 93, No. 6, 455–56.

Ekeland, E.; F. Heian; and K. B. Hagen. 2005. "Can Exercise Improve Self Esteem in Children and Young People? A Systematic Review of Randomised Controlled Trials," *British Journal of Sports Medicine*, Vol. 39, No. 11, 792–98.

Ekelund, U., and others. 2006. "Upward Weight Percentile Crossing in Infancy and Early Childhood Independently Predicts Fat Mass in Young Adults: The Stockholm Weight Development Study (SWEDES)," *American Journal of Clinical Nutrition*, Vol. 83, No. 2, 324–30.

Ekelund, U., and others. 2007. "Independent Associations of Physical Activity and Cardiorespiratory Fitness with Metabolic Risk Factors in Children: The European Youth Heart Study," *Diabetologia*, Vol. 50, No. 9, 1832–40.

Evans, J., and G. C. Roberts. 1987. "Physical Competence and the Development of Children's Peer Relations," *Quest*, Vol. 39, 23–35.

Finn, K.; N. Johannsen; and B. Specker. 2002. "Factors Associated with Physical Activity in Preschool Children," *The Journal of Pediatrics*, Vol. 140, No. 1, 81–85.

Flinchum, B. 1988. "Early Childhood Movement Programmes: Preparing Teachers for Tomorrow," *Journal of Physical Education, Recreation & Dance*, Vol. 59, No. 7, 62–64.

Folio, R. M., and R. R. Fewell. 2000. *Peabody Developmental Motor Scales* (Second edition). Austin, TX: PRO-ED Inc.

From Neurons to Neighborhoods: The Science of Early Childhood Development. 2000. Edited by J. P. Shonkoff and D. A. Phillips. Washington, DC: National Academy Press.

Gallahue, D. L. 1976. *Motor Development and Movement Experiences for Young Children.* New York: John Wiley and Sons, Inc.

Gallahue, D. L. 1982. *Developmental Movement Experiences for Children.* New York: John Wiley and Sons Inc.

Gallahue, D. L. 1995. "A Play Approach to Increased Physical Activity and Healthy Eating: With Application to Overweight and Obese Children." Paper presented at the First International Conference and Festival on Traditional Play, Games and Sport; Bangkok, Thailand.

Gallahue, D. L. 2005. "Physical Education Curriculum," in *Reaching Potentials: Transforming Early Childhood Curriculum and Assessment,* 125–43. Washington, DC: National Association for the Education of Young Children.

Gallahue, D. L., and F. Cleland-Donnelly. 2003. *Developmental Physical Education for All Children* (Fourth edition). Champaign, IL: Human Kinetics.

Gallahue, D. L., and J. C. Ozmun. 2006a. *Understanding Motor Development: Infants, Children, Adolescents, and Adults* (Sixth edition). Boston: McGraw-Hill.

Gallahue, D. L., and J. C. Ozmun. 2006b. "Motor Development in Young Children," in *Handbook of Research on the Education of Young Children* (Second edition). Edited by B. Spodek and O. N. Saracho. Mahwah, NJ: Lawrence Erlbaum Associates.

Garcia, C. 2002. "Childhood," in *Understanding Motor Development: Infants, Children, Adolescents and Adults* (Fifth edition), 161–286. Edited by D. L. Gallahue and J. C. Ozmun. Boston: McGraw Hill.

Garcia, C., and L. Garcia. 2002. "Examining Developmental Changes in Throwing: A Closeup Look," *Motor Development Research and Reviews,* Vol. 2, 62–95.

Garcia, C., and others. 2002. "Improving Public Health Through Early Childhood Movement Programs," *Journal of Physical Education, Recreation & Dance,* Vol. 73, No. 1, 27–31, 53.

Ginsburg, K. R. 2007. "The Importance of Play in Promoting Healthy Child Development and Maintaining Strong Parent-Child Bonds," *Pediatrics,* Vol. 119, No. 1, 182–91.

Goodway, J. D., and C. F. Branta. 2003. "Influence of a Motor Skill Intervention on Fundamental Motor Skill Development of Disadvantaged Preschool Children," *Research Quarterly of Exercise and Sport,* Vol. 74, No.1, 36–46.

Goodway, J. D., and D. W. Smith. 2005. "Keeping All Children Healthy: Challenges to Leading an Active Lifestyle for Preschool Children Qualifying for At-Risk Programs," *Family and Community Health,* Vol. 28, No. 2, 142–155.

Gwynne, K.; L. Hughes; and B. Blick. 1997. *The Motor Performance Checklist Manual.* Sydney: Northern Sydney Health Pubications.

Hands, B., and D. Larkin. 2006. "Physical Fitness Differences in Children With and Without Motor Learning Difficulties," *European Journal of Special Needs Education,* Vol. 21, No. 4, 447–56.

Harms, T.; R. Clifford; and D. Cryer. 2005. *Early Childhood Environment Rating Scale,* (Revised edition). New York: Teachers College Press.

Harris, S. 1996. "The Effectiveness of Early Intervention for Children with Cerebral Palsy and Related Motor Disabilites," in *The Effectiveness of Early Intervention,* 327. Edited by M. Guralnick. Baltimore: Brookes Publishing Company.

Haywood, K. M., and N. Getchell. 2005. *Life Span Motor Development* (Fourth edition). Champaign, IL: Human Kinetics.

Ignico, A. 1994. "Early Childhood Physical Education: Providing the Foundation. (Preschool Physical Education: Challenges for the Profession),"

Journal of Physical Education, Recreation & Dance, Vol. 65, No. 6, 28–30.

Isaacs, J. B. 2007. *Cost-Effective Investments in Children.* Washington, DC: The Brookings Institution.

Kohen-Raz, R. 1970. "Developmental Patterns of Static Balance Ability and Their Relation to Cognitive School Readiness," *Pediatrics,* Vol. 46, No. 2, 276–85.

Kuntzleman, C. T., and G. G. Reiff. 1992. "The Decline in American Children's Fitness Levels," *Research Quarterly of Exercise and Sport,* Vol. 63, No. 2, 107–11.

Lam, H. M. Y. 2005. "Effects of Instructional Methods on Gross Motor Proficiency of Hong Kong Preschoolers." Adelaide: University of South Australia (doctoral dissertation).

Levine, M., and E. A. Schneider. 1985. *The Pediatric Examination of Educational Readiness Examiner's Manual.* Toronto: Educators Publishing Services.

Lobo, Y. B., and A. Winsler. 2006. "The Effects of a Creative Dance and Movement Program on the Social Competence of Head Start Preschoolers," *Social Development,* Vol.15, No. 3, 501–19.

Losse, A., and others. 1991. "Clumsiness in Children—Do They Grow Out of It? A 10-year Follow-up Study," *Developmental Medicine and Child Neurology,* Vol. 33, No. 1, 55–68.

McKenzie, T. 2004. "Environment, Youth and Physical Activity." Paper presented at the 13th Annual Raymond Weiss Lecture for the Annual Convention of the American Alliance for Health, Physical Education, Recreation & Dance, New Orleans.

McKenzie, T. L., and others. 2002. "Childhood Movement Skills: Predictors of Physical Activity in Anglo American and Mexican American Adolescents?" *Research Quarterly for Exercise and Sport,* Vol. 73, No. 3, 238–44.

Miller, S. 1978. "The Facilitation of Fundamental Motor Skill Learning in Young Children." East Lansing: Michigan State University (doctoral dissertation).

Montgomery, C.; J. J. Reilly; D. M. Jackson; L. A. Kelly; C. Slater; J. Y. Paton; and S. Grant. 2004. "Relation Between Physical Activity and Energy Expenditure in a Representative Sample of Young Children," *American Journal of Clinical Nutrition* 80, No. 30, 591–96.

Nader, P. R., and others. 2006. "Identifying Risk for Obesity in Early Childhood," *Pediatrics,* Vol. 118, No. 3, 594–601.

National Association for Sport and Physical Education. 2002. *Active Start: A Statement of Physical Activity Guidelines for Children Birth to Five Years.* Reston, VA: National Association for Sport and Physical Education.

National Association for Sport and Physical Education. 2003. *Your Active Child.* Reston, VA: National Association for Sport and Physical Education.

National Association for Sport and Physical Education. 2004. *Physical Activity for Children: A Statement of Guidelines.* Reston, VA: National Association for Sport and Physical Education.

National Association for the Education of Young Children. 2005. *NAEYC Early Childhood Program Standards and Accreditation Criteria: The Mark of Quality in Early Childhood Education.* Washington, DC: National Association for the Education of Young Children.

National Center for Education in Maternal Child and Health. 2002. *Bright Futures in Practice: Physical Activity.* Washington, DC: National Center for Education in Maternal and Child Health.

Newell, K. 1984. "Physical Constraints to Development of Motor Skills," in *Motor Development During Preschool and Elementary Years,* 105–20. Edited by J. Thomas. Minneapolis, MN: Burgess.

O'Connor, J. 2000. "An Investigation Into the Hierarchical Nature of Fundamental Movement Skill Development." Melbourne: Royal Melbourne Institute of Technology (doctoral dissertation).

Ogden, C. L.; K. M. Flegel; M. D. Carroll; and C. L. Johnson. 2002. "Prevalence of Overweight Among Children and Adolescents, 1999–2000," *Journal of American Medical Association*, Vol. 288, No. 14, 1728–32.

Ortega, F. B., and others. 2008. "Physical Fitness in Childhood and Adolescence: A Powerful Marker of Health," *International Journal of Obesity*, Vol. 32, No. 1, 1–11.

Pakula, A. L., and F. B. Palmer. 1996. "Early Intervention for Children at Risk for Neuromotor Problems," in *The Effectiveness of Early Intervention*, 99. Edited by M. Guralnick. Baltimore: Brookes Publishing Company.

Parfitt, G., and R. G. Eston. 2005. "The Relationship Between Children's Habitual Activity Level and Psychological Well-being," *Acta Paediatrica*, Vol. 94, No. 12, 1791–97.

Parizkova, J. 2008. "Impact of Education on Food Behaviour, Body Composition and Physical Fitness in Children," *British Journal of Nutrition*, Vol. 99, Supplement 1, S26–32.

Pate, R. R., and others. 1996. "Tracking of Physical Activity in Young Children," *Medicine and Science in Sports and Exercise*, Vol. 28, No. 1, 92–96.

Pate, R. R., and others. 2004. "Physical Activity Among Children Attending Preschools," *Pediatrics*, Vol. 114, No. 5, 1258–63.

Payne, V. G., and L. Isaacs. 2005. *Human Motor Development: A Lifespan Approach*. Boston: McGraw-Hill.

Piek, J. P.; G. B. Baynam; and N. C. Barrett. 2006. "The Relationship Between Fine and Gross Motor Ability, Self-Perceptions and Self-Worth in Children and Adolescents," *Human Movement Science*, Vol. 25, No. 1, 65–75.

Poinsett, A. 1996. *The Role of Sports in Youth Development: Report of a Meeting Convened by Carnegie Corporation of New York*. New York: Carnegie Corporation.

Portman, P. A. 1995. "Who Is Having Fun in Physical Education Classes? Experiences of Sixth-Grade Students in Elementary and Middle Schools," *Journal of Teaching in Physical Education*, Vol. 14, No. 4, 445–53.

Reilly, J. J., and others. 2004. "Total Energy Expenditure and Physical Activity in Young Scottish Children: Mixed Longitudinal Study," *The Lancet*, Vol. 363, No. 9404, 211–12.

Reilly, J. J., and others. 2006. "Physical Activity to Prevent Obesity in Young Children: Cluster Randomised Controlled Trial," *British Medical Journal*, Vol. 333, No. 7577, 1041.

Rickard, K. A., and others. 1995a. "The Play Approach to Learning: An Alternative Paradigm for Healthy Eating and Active Play," *Pediatric Basics*, Vol. 76, 2–7.

Rickard, K. A., and others. 1995b. "The Play Approach to Learning in the Context of Families and Schools: An Alternative Paradigm for Nutrition and Fitness Education for the 21st Century," *Journal of the American Dietetic Association*, Vol. 95, No. 10, 1121–26.

Rose, B.; D. Larkin; and B. G. Berger. 1997. "Coordination and Gender Influences on the Perceived Competence of Children," *Adapted Physical Activity Quarterly*, Vol. 14, No. 3, 210–21.

Rowland, T. W. 2007. "Promoting Physical Activity for Children's Health: Rationale and Strategies," *Sports Medicine*, Vol. 37, No. 11, 929–36.

Sallis, J. F., and others. 1999. "Effects of Health-Related Physical Education on Academic Achievement: Project SPARK," *Research Quarterly for Exercise and Sport*, Vol. 70, No. 2, 127–34.

Sanders, S. 2002. *Active for Life: Developmentally Appropriate Movement Programs for Young Children.* Champaign, IL: Human Kinetics

Seefeldt, V. 1980. "Developmental Motor Patterns: Implications for Elementary School Physical Education," in *Psychology of Motor Behavior and Sport,* 314–23. Edited by C. Nadeau and others. Champaign, IL: Human Kinetics.

Skinner, R. A., and J. P. Piek. 2001. "Psychosocial Implications of Poor Motor Coordination in Children and Adolescents," *Human Movement Science,* Vol. 20, No. 1–2, 73–94.

Son, S. H. M., and S. J. Meisel. 2006. "The Relationship of Young Children's Motor Skills to Later Reading and Math Achievement," *Merrill-Palmer Quarterly,* Vol. 52, 755–78.

Telama, R., and others. 1997. "Physical Activity in Childhood and Adolescence as a Predictor of Physical Activity in Adulthood," *American Journal of Preventive Medicine,* Vol. 13, 317–23.

Timmons, B. W.; P. J. Naylor; and K. A. Pfeiffer. 2007. "Physical Activity for Preschool Children—How Much and How?" *Canadian Journal of Public Health,* Vol. 98, Supplement 2, S122–34.

Trost, S. G., and others. 2003. "Physical Activity in Overweight and Nonoverweight Preschool Children," *International Journal of Obesity,* Vol. 7, No. 7, 834–39.

Trost, S. 2007. *Physical Education, Physical Activity and Academic Performance.* San Diego: Robert Wood Johnson Foundation.

van der Meer, A. L., and F. R. van der Weel. 1999. "Development of Perception in Action in Healthy and At-Risk Children," *Acta Paediatrica,* Vol. 88, No. 429, 29–36.

van Sleuwen, B. E., and others. 2007. "Swaddling: A Systematic Review," *Pediatrics,* Vol. 120, No. 4, 1097–1106. Walkley, J., and others. 1993. "Fundamental Motor Skill Proficiency of Children," *Australian Council for Health Physical Education and Recreation,* Vol. 40, No. 3, 11–14.

Weiss, M. R. 2004. "Coaching Children to Embrace a 'Love of the Game,' "*Olympic Coach,* Vol. 16, No. 1, 15–17.

Weiss, M. R.; A. L. Smith; and M. Theeboom. 1996. "'That's What Friends Are For': Children's and Teenagers' Perceptions of Peer Relationships in the Sport Domain," *Journal of Sport and Exercise Psychology,* Vol. 18, No. 4, 347–79.

Wells, N. M., and G. W. Evans. 2003. "Nearby Nature: A Buffer of Life Stress Among Rural Children," *Environment and Behavior,* Vol. 35, No. 3, 311–30.

Williams, C. L., and others. 1998. "Healthy Start: A Comprehensive Health Education Program for Preschool Children," *Preventive Medicine,* Vol. 27, No. 2, 216–23.

Williams, C. L., and others. 2004. "Cardiovascular Risk Reduction in Preschool Children: The 'Healthy Start' Project," *Journal of the American College of Nutrition,* Vol. 23, No. 2, 117–23.

Winnick, J. P., and B. Lavay. 2005. "Perceptual-Motor Development," in *Adapted Physical Education and Sport* (Fourth edition), 359–72. Champaign, IL: Human Kinetics.

Zachopoulou, E.; A. Tsapakidou; and V. Derri. 2004. "The Effects of a Developmentally Appropriate Music and Movement Program on Motor Performance," *Early Childhood Research Quarterly,* Vol. 19, No. 4, 631–42.

Zimmer, R., and M. Volkamer. 1987. MOT 4-6. *Motoriktest fuer vier-bis sechsjaehrige kinder.* Manual. Belz: Weinheim.

FOUNDATIONS IN
Health

> "The earliest years of our lives set us on paths leading toward—or away from—good health."
>
> —Robert Wood Johnson Foundation 2008

The preschool foundations for health describe the knowledge and skills that set the groundwork for all preschool children to develop into healthy adults. The foundations describe what children should know about health when provided with high-quality education in preschool and which health habits and practices should become part of their daily routines. Those skills and behaviors set young children on the path to health and healthy lifestyle choices.

The Impact of Preschool on Children's Health

There is considerable research on the direct and indirect health benefits of comprehensive, model early childhood programs. The benefits are even more significant for children with risk factors and are evident in the outcomes: the reduced incidence of child injuries, child abuse, depression, drug use, emergency room visits, and hospitalizations; better eating habits; and improved use of health services, including health screenings and immunizations (Braveman, Sadegh-Nobariand, and Ergeter 2008). These health benefits are evident in long-term follow-up studies in adulthood. Research suggests that adults who have had a high-quality preschool experience show improved health behaviors and less depression (Palfrey and others 2005).

There is increasing recognition that health education must begin in early childhood. Health-promotion goals for preschool children at the national level include prevention of injuries and infectious diseases and improvement in nutrition and physical activity (U.S. Department of Health and Human Services 2000a). For many children, preschool offers the only opportunity for safe, vigorous outdoor play and nutritious meals. In partnership with parents, preschool programs can have an important impact on the health knowledge, skills, attitudes, and practices of the children and families they serve. In order to influence children's health, preschool professionals need to be aware of the important role they play in children's health education.

Factors Shaping Preschool Children's Health

Individual differences in personal health often begin early in life and are maintained across the life span (Guyer and others 2008). For example, risk factors for heart disease related to nutrition are common in children by age three and tend to be stable over time (Hayman and others 2004; Williams and others 1998). The United States is experiencing a growing inequality in life expectancy between its poor and wealthy citizens. This is primarily due to diseases such as lung cancer, diabetes, and heart disease. These diseases are related to health choices and to access to health care, health information, and nutritious food. These access problems are particularly acute for Californians with limited English.

By preschool, there are already large disparities in health among the children of California. California's preschool population includes increasing numbers of children with chronic health conditions and disabilities. The Maternal and Child Health Bureau defines children with special health care needs as "children who have or are at increased risk for a chronic physical, developmental, behavioral, or emotional condition and who also require health and related services of a type or amount beyond that required by children generally" (McPherson and others 1998, 138). It is estimated that about 10 percent of preschool children have special health care needs (Newacheck and others 2008). Asthma is diagnosed in 15 percent of California's children (Children Now 2009). Children living in poverty are significantly more likely to have a special health care need than their middle-class peers (Van Dyck and others 2004).

All children, but especially children with special health care needs, require a *medical home.* A medical home is a regular source of primary care that is accessible, continuous, comprehensive, family centered, coordinated, compassionate, and culturally effective (Dickens and others 1992). However, there are large disparities in the quality of medical homes for children. Children whose families are uninsured and have low incomes are least likely to have a high-quality medical home (Stevens and others 2009). Children in California whose families have low incomes are much more likely to use the emergency room and be hospitalized for asthma than middle-class children (Children Now 2009).

For all children, but especially for children with special health-care needs, the management of symptoms, the prevention of complications, and the promotion of health are critically important for educational success in preschool and beyond. This requires a partnership of parents, health-care providers, and preschool educators working together. For example, the parents, teachers, and health-care provider of a child with asthma need to work together to develop a special health-care plan. This plan outlines the child's typical symptoms, how to respond, medications used, who is responsible for storing and administering medications, and how staff will be trained in the use of inhalers and nebulizers. A well-developed special health-care plan is essential for the successful inclusion of preschool children with special health conditions.

The Role of Families in Children's Health

Preschool teachers often consider children's health a parental responsibility (Taveras and others 2006). Research supports the idea that the most common way that children learn about health is through family relationships, routines, and practices (Tinsley 2003). What children learn about health at home is shaped by their families' culture, education, attitudes, and resources. Children in California come to preschool with different experiences of access to health care (Flores and Tomany-Korman 2008) and different understandings of health and health practices. For example, some Chinese and Puerto Rican families balance "hot" and "cold" foods in order to prevent sickness and disease, and the foods they choose for their children will reflect these beliefs.

Access to health care, fresh fruit and vegetables, open space for play, and physical activity is limited for many families (Flores and Tomany-Korman 2008; Henrickson, Smith, and Eikenberry 2006; Popkin, Duffey, and Gordon-Larsen 2005). Parents' long working hours can result in limited time to prepare nutritious meals or to engage in physical activities with their children. Preschool educators need to be aware that children in California come to preschool with a variety of understandings of health and health practices. The diverse cultures of the children need to be respected by educators teaching about health and health practices. Sharing information about health and health practices with families is a valuable aspect of preschool education. Strategies for working effectively with parents and families on health are addressed in the *California Preschool Curriculum Framework, Volume 2* (forthcoming).

The Role of Preschool in Children's Health

Parenting practices, access to health care, and socioeconomic status play a large role in children's health, but the important role of preschool programs in children's health should not be underestimated. Children spend longer hours in the care of teachers and caregivers today than they did in the past (Savage, Fisher, and Birch 2007). On average, children under age five with working mothers spend 36 hours a week in child care (NACCRRA 2008). This finding means that many children with working mothers spend as much weekday time in the care of child care providers and preschool teachers as they do with their parents. Children in full-time child care programs get one-half to two-thirds of their daily calorie requirements met in child care. Busy parents working long hours often depend on child care and preschool professionals to teach healthy nutritional practices to their children (American Dietetic Association 2005). This reality highlights the importance of addressing health in the preschool setting, where an impact can be made on the lives of many children.

Forty-five percent of children with a chronic illness are reported to fall behind in school (Thies 1999). Healthy children are more likely to attend school and to succeed in school (Blumenshine and others 2008; Kramer, Allen, and Gergen 1995; Spernak and others 2006; Wolfe 1985). Health, in turn, influences children's ability to be physically active and to learn more effectively. Preschool educators are in a unique position to influence the health knowledge, skills, attitudes, and practices of the children in their care (Gupta and others 2005; Hughes and others 2007; Taveras and others 2006). In partnership with parents, preschool teachers can model healthy behaviors and help to instill in preschool children health habits with the potential to influence their health for a lifetime.

Children in preschool settings develop health knowledge, skills, attitudes, and habits through everyday routines and activities. Health routines and habits can be learned and demonstrated by children who speak any language, when the behaviors are modeled and encouraged by caring adults who understand the importance of establishing these routines. Preschool children likely learn more about health from participating in and observing everyday, routine health-related practices and interactions than they would from direct instruction about health. Through participation in preschool, all children (particularly children at risk) can gain access to nutritious foods and safe outdoor place spaces, the opportunity to make healthy food choices, and the chance to participate in regular physical activity.

Many health-related behaviors, such as making healthy eating choices, engaging in physical activity, maintaining personal safety, and maintaining oral health, are well established by (or have their beginnings in) early childhood (Hahn and others 2000; Savage, Fisher, and Birch 2007; Williams and others 1998). Young children learn healthy and unhealthy habits from observing and imitating adults and other children, both at home and at preschool. Preschool educators can model and encourage healthy habits and practices that children can adopt and use for a lifetime.

The Ability to Reason About Health Concepts

It is important to read the preschool foundations for health with an understanding of what is currently known about preschool children's cognitive development and their ability to reason about health concepts. What follows is a general description of preschool children's reasoning about health concepts, followed by research findings about what children understand and can do in basic hygiene, oral health, knowledge of wellness, sun safety, injury prevention, and nutrition.

Preschool children have a limited understanding of the processes of cause and effect and how to prevent illnesses and injuries. It is important to keep this in mind when the preschool program identifies the developmentally appropriate health concepts, skills, and behaviors that young children can realistically be expected to master in the preschool years. Although preschool children's ability to reason about health and illness may limit their ability to practice preventive health behaviors (which requires more advanced causal thinking), preschool is the time when children can establish the routine practices and habits that provide the groundwork for a healthy lifestyle. This is particularly true for nutrition, physical activity, oral health, and injury prevention.

Piaget and his colleagues developed influential theories of what children understand about health and illness (see the Bibliographic Notes). Although Piaget's theories were an important starting point, more recent theorists argue that young children are more competent in their understandings of health and illness than Piaget and his colleagues believed. Those more recent theorists believe that children understand health concepts but may not be able to articulate this understanding well. Those experts argue that children's understanding of health is not rigidly governed by age-specific stages and that even very young children have intuitive theories about health and illness. Children's theories may be shaped by their experiences, cultural and familial contexts, and personalities (Eiser 1989; Tinsley 2003). When presented with different reasons why an individual became sick or might get sick, preschool children tend to choose explanations that are accurate, reasonable, or involve physical causes such as germs and contamination (Kalish 1996; Siegal 1988; Springer and Ruckel 1992).

There are important changes in children's ability to reason about health concepts between the ages of four and six. Preschool children do construct an intuitive biological concept of living things, but it is typically restricted to persons and animals rather than all living things. It is not until around age six that children are able to understand the role of body functions in maintaining life or the concept of a life cycle (Slaughter, Jaakkola, and Carey 1999). A more general concept of "life," or animate versus inanimate things, forms the core of their understanding of the body at the preschool level. This concept of life, or aliveness, drives preschoolers' beginning understanding of body parts and their functions, which they understand simply and very incompletely as helping to maintain life. Children begin to use functional explanations of internal body parts, although at first these explanations may be very general or not correct. Most four-year-olds respond to questions about the role of internal body parts with global and general explanations or no explanation at all (for example, *my heart keeps me alive*). This core concept of life, a product of cognitive development, is the necessary scaffolding (Vygotsky 1978) for teaching young children about their bodies and keeping them healthy for life. As their ability to think causally develops in the elementary school years, children will eventually also develop a much more detailed understanding of their internal body parts and how each part contributes to maintaining life and health.

It is unclear how much children's reasoning about health and illness can be improved with instruction. It is possible that a high-quality preschool curriculum may facilitate developmental changes in reasoning about health and health behaviors (Goldman and others 1991; Williams and Binnie 2002). Teaching preschool children about the connections between the causes and symptoms of illness may support the development of the reasoning abilities necessary to adopt positive health behaviors. Carey (1985) argues that the more knowledge about a given topic a child has, the better equipped the child is to build schemas for understanding that topic.

Before children develop a "life concept," practicing *scripts* or rules of behavior can be used to establish certain health-promoting behaviors or habits. For example, an early study (Poche, McCubbrey, and Munn 1988) on teaching three- and four-year-old children how to brush their teeth divided the task up into 16 discrete steps. Children were taught how to perform each step in order over a period of several weeks. These children were able to learn how to brush their teeth effectively and retained the skill several months after the instruction ended (Poche, McCubbrey, and Munn 1988). Such habits can provide the scaffolding for the child's developing theories about and understanding of the body, health, and life (Eiser 1989; Nelson and Gruendel 1986). For instance, children can be taught a script for buckling the seat belt when they get in their car seat. Although they do not understand the risk to their lives if they fail to follow this script, compliance is achieved because a trusted adult tells them "this is what we do." Later, school-age children begin to understand that injuries to their bodies can be life-threatening. They begin to understand the cause-and-effect concept of an accident leading to bodily injury. They can then incorporate their notion of preserving life into their car-seat script.

Young children also perform hygiene routines because a trusted adult tells them to. They do not have the goal of preventing disease, as this requires a level of cognitive development most preschoolers have not yet achieved. To achieve a feeling of mastery, or to get recognition from their teachers or family members, children establish habits that become more or less automatic depending on the environment. Later, when their ability to understand cause and effect is further developed in elementary school and beyond, children will also practice these habits because they understand the role health habits play in preventing illness.

Health-Related Practices and Routines in Preschool

Since many children lack a clear understanding of how germs cause disease, it is important to use *scripts* or rules of behavior in the preschool setting (for instance, washing hands at certain times or coughing into one's elbow). Through modeling and instruction, teachers can help children establish health practices and routines. Following these scripts will affect children's health for a lifetime. Making the behaviors automatic for a preschool child sets the stage for lifelong healthy habits. Preschool children are eager to master routines and skills. Preschool is an ideal time to begin shaping children's health habits, routines, and practices even if children do not yet grasp how their behaviors affect health.

Warm and caring adults can facilitate children's internalization of health habits. By practicing these habits, children may eventually be motivated to engage in health practices to protect their own health. For example, one study found that children of warm, nurturing mothers are more independent in a variety of health behaviors such as toothbrushing and handwashing (Lees and Tinsley 1998). This is consistent with the finding that a child will perform cognitive tasks better when she feels emotionally supported (Fischer 1980). Preschool programs in which children are taught health behaviors in a warm, nurturing environment and are encouraged to be more independent in those behaviors may directly contribute to and extend children's knowledge and skills in the health domain. This principle is especially true for children with special needs or chronic health conditions that make healthy habits and choices very important for reducing, managing, or preventing disabilities later in life.

Oral Health

Oral health is a fundamental component of general health. Early childhood *caries* (tooth decay) is the single most common chronic childhood disease in the United States (U.S. Department of Health and Human Services 200b). Approximately 40 percent of California's children are not receiving the oral health services they need (Children Now 2009). Poor oral health can affect nutrition, growth, and development. Oral health is more than just maintaining healthy teeth. The oral structures and tissues allow everyone to speak and smile, smell, taste, touch, chew, and swallow. The mouth is a point of entry for infectious organisms into the body. Children with oral infections have more ear infections, sinus infections, and infected abrasions from bumps and scrapes (Dental Health Foundation 2006). Recent research has shown associations between oral infections and diabetes; heart disease; stroke; and preterm low birth weight babies (Blumenshine and others 2008).

Oral health is particularly important for some children with disabilities. For instance, in children with physical disabilities, particularly cerebral palsy, facial muscles may affect the way that upper and lower teeth fit together. Misalignment can make toothbrushing more challenging. Children with physical disabilities often need adaptive toothbrushes and help with practicing toothbrushing. Some medications may affect tooth development and can damage tooth enamel. Good oral health for children with disabilities requires a partnership between parents, teachers, and dental professionals.

Intervention studies with preschool children show significant improvements in dental caries and oral health (Curnow and others 2002; Rong and others 2003; Wennhall and others 2005). National standards for early care and education programs include oral health and toothbrushing in the criteria for quality programs. For example, the National Association for the Education of Young Children (NAEYC) accreditation criteria specify that programs that serve two or more meals must provide at least one opportunity daily for children older than one year to clean and brush teeth (2005). Preschool children, with supervision, can be expected to brush their teeth. The extent of their ability to connect brushing their teeth with prevention of caries (see the Glossary) largely depend on their level of cognitive development. Many children will not be able to connect toothbrushing with the prevention of caries until elementary school. Helping preschool children make toothbrushing a routine habit is an important step in preventing oral health disease in children. For children in part-day programs, toothbrushing can be practiced on tooth models, songs for brushing teach can be taught, and children can be encouraged to brush their teeth at home. Parents can be offered information about the importance of oral health starting early in life. They are encouraged to make toothbrushing a regular practice at home before children begin school and at bedtime, especially in programs that do not include toothbrushing in their daily routines.

Injuries

Injuries are the leading cause of death in children over one year of age in California. The most common nonfatal injuries in the preschool age group are falls (from playground equipment, stairs, windows), being struck by or against an object or person, bites or stings, poisoning, and choking on food or a foreign body. Transportation-related injuries and drownings are the most common cause of fatal injuries (Borse and others 2008; Children's Safety Network National Resource Center n.d.).

There is interest among professionals and families in educating young children in order to prevent injuries. However, there is limited evidence in the literature that preschool children can be taught how to keep themselves safe from harmful substances or situations. Preschoolers are still developing an understanding of cause-and-effect. They are still learning whether an object or situation is likely to cause them harm and how they can respond to prevent harm to themselves. Therefore, preschool children's ability to learn about safety and change their behavior to prevent injuries is limited. Preschool children may be able to repeat lessons learned about safety, such as rules for crossing streets safely. However, when confronted with actual situations in which they are crossing the street, they are often unable to inhibit their inclination to act and may not do what they have been taught. This is particularly true for children who may act impulsively in certain situations.

Preschool children still require close supervision by adults to keep them safe. Child care providers can teach children concepts of pedestrian safety or poison prevention, but these subjects should be approached with the idea of introducing *scripts,* or rules of behavior. Scripts can inform routines and provide understanding of "what we do" in certain situations. Generally, children learn best in their everyday routines and activities; this principle applies to introducing scripts in early childhood programs. Creating a meaningful context for learning is important. Those scripts will eventually be incorporated into children's developing ability to understand why we do them. Scripts will also be incorporated into children's developing theories of life, health, and prevention of injury and illness.

Nutrition

There is substantial evidence that preschool children understand the basic concepts of nutrition. Most preschool children know that food is something that makes their bodies grow, gives them energy, and keeps them healthy. They can be taught to name the basic food groups and give examples of each. Nevertheless, preschoolers do not know how each food group contributes to their health, nor do they have a biological understanding of how food is transformed in their bodies. Young children either think that the food itself travels to different parts of the body and has an immediate effect on physical functioning, or they think that their bodies directly absorb energy from food (Inagaki and Hatano 2004). Their limited ability to understand cause-and-effect makes it difficult for preschool children to understand the long-term consequences of eating foods that are high in carbohydrates, fat, and sugar. Instead, preschoolers can learn to identify healthy and unhealthy foods when taught by parents and teachers. Like adults, however, their behavior often does not reflect what they know.

Early childhood is a critical period for children's development of food preferences. Young children who taste new foods repeatedly without being forced to eat them will acquire a taste for the new foods and learn to like them. It may take 10 to 16 exposures before a child will indicate a preference for a new food (Sullivan and Birch 1990). Early exposure prepares a child for better eating habits for a lifetime, as early food choices are predictive of adult food preferences (Rozin and Vollmecke 1986).

Preschool children need to regulate their food intake (Satter 2007; Savage, Fisher, and Birch 2007). Infants are born with the ability to self-regulate their food intake. Well-meaning adults often use feeding practices aimed at encouraging or discouraging children to eat, such as coaxing, coercion, or bribery (even those encouraging children to eat fruit and vegetables). These practices cause children to learn to respond to the external cues of adults rather than to their own internal cues of hunger and fullness, and they lose the ability to self-regulate what they eat. Research shows that preschool children who have lost the ability to respond to internal cues of fullness can be taught to identify when they are full and when they are hungry (Johnson 2000). Helping children identify when they are full and hungry is an important part of nutrition education in the preschool setting where meals are served.

Best practices suggest that meals and snacks be offered family style. Programs that get their food in single-serving portions or packaged from central kitchens can request "bulk food delivery." In this way, they provide family-style meals and are encouraged to do so by the Child Care Food Program. To preserve children's ability to self-regulate their food intake, programs should allow children to serve themselves a variety of foods in family-style meal settings. At a minimum, preschool program staff should practice what Satter (2007) calls the "division of responsibility" between the caregiver and the child: it is the caregiver's responsibility to provide appropriate, healthy foods and a safe and nurturing feeding environment. It is the child's responsibility to decide when and how much to eat. For children who bring their food from home, it is still their own responsibility to choose how much and what they eat.

These recommended best practices are complicated by the fact that 10 percent of California's families have *food insecurity* (see the Glossary). Families who have food insecurity tend to purchase lower-cost foods that are calorie-dense to prevent hunger, but those foods are also higher in starches, sugar, salt, and fats. Children raised with food insecurity have poorer health than those with food security and are at greater risk of becoming overweight or obese (Cook and Frank 2008). Food insecurity may foster the tendency to eat greater amounts when food is plentiful (for example, in preschool), disrupting children's ability to self-regulate. Some cultures discourage young children's independence in choosing their food. Preschool programs will need to work with parents to reach a common understanding about nutrition that recognizes what is known about caregivers' feeding practices, children's eating habits, and cultural practices and meanings.

Mealtime is important for children's social-emotional development as well as for nutrition. Modeling healthy eating and talking to children about the qualities of foods at mealtimes is more helpful than encouraging children to eat healthy foods. In this kind of environment, preschool children can be expected to try a variety of healthy foods, gradually acquire an appetite for ones they might not initially like, find pleasure in food and mealtimes, recognize when they are full, and maintain a healthy body weight. Family-style mealtimes are linked to cognitive development, as children have opportunities for elaborated talk and reasoning about complex concepts.

The Health Foundations

The preschool health foundations are grouped into three strands: Health Habits, Safety, and Nutrition. Health Habits cover the substrands of Basic Hygiene, Oral Health, and Sun Safety. Safety comprises the substrand of Injury Prevention. Nutrition consists of the substrands of Nutrition Knowledge, Nutrition Choices, and Self-Regulation of Eating.

Within each substrand, the foundations describe the knowledge and skills most children demonstrate at around 48 months and around 60 months of age. Although the foundations describe knowledge and skills at around 48 and 60 months of age, it is important to understand that they are age-related and not age-dependent. The foundations are illustrated by examples that put the behavior in context. Examples offer a sampling of what the foundation might look like as seen through children's behavior. When examples are given that indicate verbal expression, the child may use any language, including American Sign Language.

Bibliographic notes are provided later in this section and offer the research sources for this chapter. How to support the development of children's knowledge, skills, and behaviors related to health is addressed in the *California Preschool Curriculum Framework, Volume 2* (forthcoming).

Overview of the Foundations

Health Habits

1.0 Basic Hygiene
   1.1, 1.2
2.0 Oral Health
   2.1
3.0 Knowledge of Wellness
   3.1, 3.2, 3.3
4.0 Sun Safety
   4.1

Safety

1.0 Injury Prevention
   1.1, 1.2, 1.3

Nutrition

1.0 Nutrition Knowledge
   1.1
2.0 Nutrition Choices
   2.1, 2.2
3.0 Self-Regulation of Eating
   3.1

Health Habits

1.0 Basic Hygiene

At around 48 months of age	At around 60 months of age
1.1 Demonstrate knowledge of some steps in the handwashing routine.	**1.1** Demonstrate knowledge of more steps in the handwashing routine.
Examples	**Examples**
• Shows a friend how to wash hands but leaves out several steps. • Washes fingers and part of hand. Does not wash between fingers. • A child with Down syndrome puts soap on hands and with teacher's hands guiding her, rubs hands together, rinses, and turns off the water.	• Shows a friend how to wash hands but may leave out a step. • During toileting, a child shows a friend how to wash hands properly while singing the handwashing song. Then communicates, "Oops! I forgot to dry my hands." • After using the bathroom, a child who is nonverbal goes to the sink and follows all the directions for washing hands, pointing to each picture prompt.
1.2 Practice health habits that prevent infectious diseases and infestations (such as lice) when appropriate, with adult support, instruction, and modeling.	**1.2** Begin to independently practice health habits that prevent infectious disease and infestations (such as lice) when appropriate, with less adult support, instruction, and modeling.
Examples	**Examples**
• When reminded, coughs in sleeve, blows nose in tissue, or avoids touching blood. • When reminded, washes hands before helping to prepare snack, after using the bathroom, and before eating. • Follows rules for not sharing hats, forks, and toothbrushes, with adult support. • Drinks from a drinking fountain without touching mouth to spout, when reminded by an adult. • Washes hands after handling classroom pet, when reminded by teacher.	• When coughing during circle time, coughs into sleeve. • Sneezes while playing, gets a tissue to blow nose, throws it in the waste basket when finished, and then washes hands when prompted. • Watching a friend pick up an apple slice from the floor, communicates, "Eating dirty food can make you sick." • Tells friend not to use own spoon to serve self from common serving dish. • Drinks water from a drinking fountain without touching the spout.

2.0 Oral Health

At around 48 months of age	At around 60 months of age
2.1 Demonstrate knowledge of some steps of the routine for brushing teeth, with adult supervision and instruction.	**2.1** Demonstrate knowledge of more steps of the routine for brushing and when toothbrushing should be done, with less adult supervision.
Examples	**Examples**
• After teacher demonstrates, uses toothbrush to brush outer teeth and then spits. • Brushes teeth after mealtimes, when prompted, needing help to apply toothpaste. • After finishing breakfast, takes adaptive toothbrush, begins to make brushing motion in mouth, rinses the brush, and communicates, "Done!" • Picks up toothbrush and communicates, "I only use my own to brush my teeth."	• Applies a smear of toothpaste from own tube or from a piece of wax paper, brushes all three sides of the teeth (outsides, insides, and chewing surfaces), brushes tongue, rinses and spits, with adult guidance. • Communicates, "I brush my teeth when I wake up and when I go to bed." • Goes to the block center and asks a friend who finished eating lunch, "You didn't brush. ¿Por qué (why)?"

82 | Health Habits

3.0 Knowledge of Wellness

At around 48 months of age	*At around 60 months of age*
3.1 Identify a few internal body parts (most commonly the bones, brain, and heart) but may not understand their basic function.	**3.1** Identify several different internal body parts and demonstrate a basic, limited knowledge of some functions.

Examples | **Examples**

- Communicates "Food goes into my tummy."
- After riding tricycle, tells another child, "Feel my heart. It's beating fast!"
- When asked what the brain does, responds, "You need to have a brain to be smart."

- Touches own chest, takes a big breath, exhales, and says, "Lungs help us breathe."
- Communicates that the heart pumps blood, which keeps people alive.
- Communicates, "My bones help me move."
- Holds head and communicates, "I can't think, teacher; my brain is tired."

| **3.2** Begin to understand that health-care providers try to keep people well and help them when they are not well. | **3.2** Demonstrate greater understanding that health-care providers try to keep people well and help them when they are not well. |

Examples | **Examples**

- While in dramatic play area, pretends to be a doctor and communicates that medicine will make people feel better.
- Explains that dentists take care of teeth and that doctors and nurses give medicine to make sick people well.
- In the dramatic play area, acts the part of doctor and puts a bandage on a friend's pretend "owee."

- Communicates that the doctor or nurse may give a shot or pill or medicine to help keep them well.
- Child with diabetes explains that the school nurse helps her with her insulin.
- Communicates, "My dentist says I need to brush my teeth after eating candy."

| **3.3** Communicate to an adult about not feeling well, feeling uncomfortable, or about a special health need, with varying specificity and reliability. | **3.3** Communicate to an adult about not feeling well, feeling uncomfortable, or about a special health need, with more specificity and reliability. |

Examples | **Examples**

- Child with asthma having symptoms communicates, "My tummy hurts," rather than "I can't breathe."
- Tells teacher, "Peanuts make me sick."
- Communicates, "My tummy hurts" when noticing need to have a bowel movement.
- Tells the teacher, "I wear a special bracelet because sugar makes me sick."

- Child with asthma starts to wheeze and says to teacher, "I need my asthma medicine."
- Communicates to the teacher, "I can't eat peanuts because I am allergic to them."
- Tells teacher, "My head hurts; I need to lie down."
- Deaf child lets adult know that hearing aid is not working by pointing to his ear or saying "It's broken."
- Tells the teacher, "I wear a special bracelet because I have diabetes."

4.0 Sun Safety

At around 48 months of age	At around 60 months of age
4.1 Begin to practice sun-safe actions, with adult support and guidance.	**4.1** Practice sun-safe actions with decreasing adult support and guidance.
Examples	**Examples**
• Allows adult to apply sunscreen before going outside, as requested by the parent. • Seeks shade in outdoor play area with adult guidance and supervision. • Gets a drink of water during active outdoor play when invited by the teacher. • Goes to cubby and takes a sun hat to wear when going out to the playground and prompted by an adult.	• Before going outside, says, "It's sunny out; I need my hat," and puts on own hat. • After playing tag on the play yard, communicates, "I'm thirsty" and gets a drink of water. • Sometimes seeks shade or sunscreen without being told by an adult.

Safety

1.0 Injury Prevention

At around 48 months of age	At around 60 months of age
1.1 Follow safety rules with adult support and prompting.	**1.1** Follow safety rules more independently though may still need adult support and prompting.
Examples	**Examples**
• Follows the rule to walk when inside the classroom, though may need a reminder when excited. • With prompting by an adult, uses own helmet when riding a wheeled toy. • Reminds another child, "Teacher said, 'don't throw sand.'" • Slides feet first down the slide with adult supervision and prompting.	• Stays a safe distance from children riding wheeled toys. • Checks to make sure the bottom of the slide is clear before sliding down. • Uses own helmet and buckles the chin strap most of the time when riding a wheeled toy. • Holds up one hand and says, "*Alto* (stop)!" when another child is running in the classroom.
1.2 Begin to show ability to follow emergency routines after instruction and practice (for example, a fire drill or earthquake drill).	**1.2** Demonstrate increased ability to follow emergency routines after instruction and practice.
Examples	**Examples**
• Acts out in the dramatic play area by calling for help (for example, 911), pretending there is an emergency. • Follows teacher's instructions to line up and exit the building during a fire drill.	• At circle time, communicates that 911 is the number to call if someone is hurt and people should shout "fire" when noticing a fire and should run outside. • Lines up with adult guidance, according to practiced routine, when the teacher announces that it is an emergency.
1.3 Show beginning ability to follow transportation and pedestrian safety rules with adult instruction and supervision.	**1.3** Show increased ability to follow transportation and pedestrian safety rules with adult support and supervision.
Examples	**Examples**
• After instruction, stops at the curb and looks at an adult to be sure it is safe to cross. • Keeps wheelchair between white lines at crosswalk when prompted by an adult. • Sees a stop sign, when on a walk in the neighborhood, and communicates to the group, "Stop."	• Modeling an accompanying adult, stops at the curb, looks both ways, and keeps looking for cars while crossing, staying within lines of crosswalk. • In dramatic play area, tells a doll "Let's buckle up in the car seat before we go to the store."

Nutrition

1.0 Nutrition Knowledge

At around 48 months of age	At around 60 months of age
1.1 Identify different kinds of foods.	**1.1** Identify a larger variety of foods and may know some of the related food groups.
Examples	**Examples**
• A visually impaired child reaches into a bag of fruits and vegetables, selects one, and says, "This is a soft banana." • After working in class garden, names foods that are grown in the ground. • In the dramatic play area, children talk about their favorite types of fruit. A child says, "My mom always buys lots of mangoes. I eat them every day."	• Selects foods from two food groups at the snack table and comments, "I picked two kinds of food: an apple and string cheese." • Describes what a green bean feels like and what it is and identifies it as a vegetable when touching one inside a bag. • Says strawberries and blueberries are both berries and tells other children how she picked them.

2.0 Nutrition Choices

At around 48 months of age	*At around 60 months of age*
2.1 Demonstrate a beginning understanding that eating a variety of food helps the body grow and be healthy, and choose from a variety of foods at mealtimes.	**2.1** Demonstrate greater understanding that eating a variety of food helps the body grow and be healthy, and choose from a greater variety of foods at mealtimes.
Examples	**Examples**
<ul><li>During a family-style meal, self-serves broccoli and carrots, and communicates, "This makes me strong!" while flexing arm muscle.</li><li>States, "I like tofu and cabbage, just like my mom."</li><li>Chooses a serving of a familiar food at lunch and a small taste of a new food, such as kiwi, that the teacher describes as full of vitamins and helpful to the body.</li><li>Places the serving bowl on another child's wheelchair tray and asks, "Do you want some fruit salad on your plate?"</li></ul>	<ul><li>When getting food during a family-style meal, pours milk and communicates: "I drink milk to keep my bones strong. And I eat carrots to help me see better!"</li><li>Packs an imaginary lunch using many different kinds of healthy food while playing in the play kitchen area.</li><li>Communicates, "My teacher says this snack is healthy. It has bananas and apples."</li><li>Communicates, "Teacher, my grandma made me chicken, rice, and corn because it keeps me healthy."</li></ul>
2.2 Indicate food preferences that reflect familial and cultural practices.	**2.2** Indicate food preferences based on familial and cultural practices and on some knowledge of healthy choices.
Examples	**Examples**
<ul><li>In a discussion about breads, children look at a basket of plastic breads from all over the world, such as bagels, matzos, pita, and croissant. One child says, "Steamed buns are like Chinese bread! They're really soft!" Another child says, "My mom makes Irish soda bread!"</li><li>Says at group time, "I like tamales. My mom, daddy, grandma, aunt, and me all help to make them."</li><li>While seated at the table, a child says, "I have rice porridge for breakfast. It's my favorite. " Another child says, "I have grits for breakfast. I have it with scrambled eggs." Another child says, "I have oatmeal for breakfast."</li><li>Identifies special foods eaten on holidays (for example, Chanukah) or special occasions: "My daddy made me a *licuado de papaya* (papaya shake)."</li><li>Tells a friend who is eating a chicken sandwich at lunch, "I am not supposed to eat chicken. Nobody in my family eats chicken."</li></ul>	<ul><li>Enjoys eating green beans grown in the class garden with friends and lets others know, "I helped grow these veggies. They're good for us."</li><li>After reading Grace Lin's book, *The Ugly Vegetable Soup,* children and their teacher follow the recipe provided in the book, make the soup, and enjoy it. Some children ask to borrow the book so that their parents can make the soup for them at home.</li><li>After helping to peel hard-boiled eggs, tangerines, and bananas for snack and talking with teacher about why they are nutritious, chooses eggs and tangerines for own snack, proudly indicating "I peeled these!"</li><li>At lunchtime, a child avoids milk and says, "Milk makes my stomach feel bad. I drink soy milk."</li><li>When asked what vegetables they would like to grow in their class garden, one child communicates bok choy; another says, tomatoes; and a third one says peas; and a fourth says collard greens.</li><li>At lunchtime, a child chooses to drink pineapple juice rather than apple or orange juice and says, "We always have pineapple juice in my house. It's good for me!"</li></ul>

3.0 Self-Regulation of Eating

At around 48 months of age	At around 60 months of age
3.1 Indicate awareness of own hunger and fullness.	**3.1** Indicate greater awareness of own hunger and fullness.
Examples	**Examples**
• Arrives in the morning and communicates, "I'm hungry; I want some breakfast!" • When offered a piece of banana, communicates, "I ate some, and now I'm full." • At lunch, deaf child signs, "No more; I'm full," and passes the bowl of fruit along to another child.	• Says, "When I get hungry, I ask Mommy for something to eat." • At snack time communicates, "I'm not hungry any more so I'm going to go play." • When reading *The Very Hungry Caterpillar,* communicates, "Eating all of that would make me *really* full."

Bibliographic Notes

Health Habits

Basic Hygiene

Through basic hygiene, preschool children link their actions with protecting and promoting their health. An interview study of healthy preschool children (Goldman and others 1991) found that preschool-age children have difficulty understanding that their actions might contribute to becoming ill, but they do seem to understand that they can play an active role in recovering from illness. For example, children in the study said that going to the doctor and taking medicine were ways to get well when they were sick.

Handwashing is a fundamental process related to basic hygiene. It is also a basic health habit. A study of a handwashing curriculum for preschool children and their caregivers showed that children's handwashing techniques and the frequency and willingness with which they washed their hands improved as a result of the curriculum (Niffenegger 1997). A study of an intervention examining the effect of a handwashing curriculum on three- and four-year-old preschool children found that children at those ages have very low rates of handwashing (Rosen and others 2006). The rates improved with instruction and practice but only to about 60 percent before meals and about 50 percent after bathroom use. The intervention included training the educators, providing an educational program for the children, providing home education, collaborating with school nurses, installing soap and paper-towel dispensers, and providing liquid soap. Such studies show the importance of handwashing in the preschool setting and the value of teacher support for children to build the habit of handwashing.

Oral Health

Research on oral health education for U.S. preschool children is limited. In a 2003 study in China (Rong and others 2003), in which children and parents were given information and instruction in oral health, children in the intervention group had significantly better oral health and reported brushing their teeth twice a day and before bedtime. A similar study in Sweden (Wennhall and others 2005) investigated the effectiveness of an oral health program, including parent education and toothbrush training for two- to three-year-old preschool children living in a multicultural, low-socioeconomic area. The study found significantly reduced caries in the intervention group. Those studies show the possibilities for improvement in children's oral health from education and practice in the preschool setting.

Knowledge of Wellness

Piaget and Piagetian theorists have been influential in the training of early childhood educators. Bibace and Walsh (1980) developed a theory of children's understanding of illness based on Piaget's theory of cognitive development. According to Bibace and Walsh's theory, preschoolers, who are in the *preoperational stage* of cognitive

development, are not yet able to clearly distinguish between cause and effect. Because of what Piaget referred to as *precausal reasoning,* Bibace and Walsh argue that young children will base their explanations of illness simply on physical and temporal proximity. This means that whatever is close to a person in time or space will be identified as the cause of an illness. For example, if someone asks a child how he got sick, he might respond, "From the cold wind in my face" or "From the sun."

However, recent research into children's understanding of health and illness suggests that children do have intuitive theories of health and illness. Moreover, the studies suggest that these theories are not rigidly governed by age-specific stages. For instance, Kalish (1996, 1999) argues that young children do not understand the biological basis of infection, but they do understand that contagion is a physical process. Rather than assuming, as Piaget claimed, that contagion merely reflects an association between two objects or ideas (for example, "I got sick from the sun"), Kalish suggests that young children expect contagion and contamination to rely on some physical entity that is transferred. Preschool children recognize that people who sneeze, for instance, could not make others sick unless they sneezed on them. This intuitive understanding, coupled with the everyday health practices and routines that a child learns in the preschool years, provides the scaffolding for the child's later development of a biologically based understanding of infection and illness.

The model of infection held by many Western adults treats germs as the physical carriers of disease. Studies show that although preschool children expect disease to result from physical causes, children's understanding of germs is not consistent. Some children recognize that germs are tiny, invisible things that can hurt people. Other children know nothing about germs or are confused by adult references to germs as "bugs" (Wilkinson 1988).

Preschool children have difficulty grasping the abstract concept of health. The concept of prevention requires an application of causal reasoning that is difficult for preschoolers. Koopman and colleagues (2004) found that children below eleven years of age will have difficulty in understanding the reason for an instruction when it concerns an *internal* bodily process; for instance, that eating a low-fat diet will prevent heart disease. Kalnins and Love (1982) report that children at all ages think of health as a state arising from following a series of practices or rules that include eating proper food, getting exercise, and keeping clean. Children's health concepts are related to their age or stage, personality, family background, experience, and health.

Preschool children have a less differentiated sense of the inside of their bodies than older children do. They do not know many internal parts. When asked to label what is inside them, they are just as likely to mention something permanent (for example, bones) as something impermanent (for example, what they ate for lunch). Similarly, the concept of illness prevention is difficult for preschool children to understand. Preschool children understand that food is necessary for health and growth, but they have a poor understanding of how the body processes the food that they eat. As children develop better causal reasoning, their ability to understand illness prevention also increases. Coppens (1985) found that those preschool children in her study with better causal reasoning were better able to differentiate between safe and unsafe situations and to identify preventive measures for avoiding injury or harm.

Sun Safety

An evaluation study of a sun-safety curriculum taught to preschool children found that children who received instruction to ask for sunscreen, cover up, and find shade showed improved understanding of these safety practices. Children did not translate this knowledge, however, into their behavior in new situations (Loescher and others 1995).

Nonetheless, Loescher and others (1995) argue that health education efforts are still important at this age because they help children become more cooperative with caregivers' sun-safety efforts. Similarly, a study of five- to ten-year-olds found that a sun-safety curriculum increased awareness of sun-safe behaviors, but the transfer of that awareness to the playground was not significant (McWhirter and others 2000).

In California, Community Care Licensing regulations require written permission by parents before sunscreen may be applied to children in early childhood programs *(California Code of Regulations,* Title 22, Section 101226). Many programs do not make applying sunscreen a routine practice because of this requirement. *Caring for Our Children* (American Academy of Pediatrics 2002) and the NAEYC accreditation standards recommend the use of sunscreen, with parental permission, in early childhood programs. This is an especially important practice in the preschool population since young children are not able to behave in a way that follows recommendations on sun safety. The incidence of skin cancer is rising rapidly due largely to sun exposure, particularly sun exposure in childhood. When properly applied, sunscreens are effective in the prevention of skin cancer (MacNeal and Dinulos 2007).

Safety

Despite improved education and prevention initiatives, injury remains the leading cause of death in children over one year of age and exceeds all other causes of death combined (Mendelson and Fallat 2007). Research shows that many preschool children are not able to consistently identify dangerous situations. They are also often not able to generate preventive responses in such situations. Making judgments about how likely they are to be injured or harmed by their behavior or by a situation is difficult for them (Hardy 2002).

Injury Prevention

Knowledge of safety emerges in children before they are able to take action to prevent injury (Coppens 1985). Children can learn about safety; for instance, they can learn rules about not running in the street or that it is not safe to jump from the top of the play structure. Children can state those rules. But they cannot reliably follow those rules and use them, when in an unsafe situation, in order to prevent an injury from happening.

Young children's knowledge about safety is quite variable and cannot be relied upon to serve a protective function for them. In a study (Morrongiello, Midgett, and Shields 2001) of the relationship between safety-rule knowledge and injury rates in preschool children, researchers found no relationship between safety knowledge and injury rate in four- to six-year-olds. Knowing a rule does not ensure that a preschool child will act consistently with what he or she knows. At this age, adult supervision is still an important factor in terms of injury prevention (Morrongiello, Midgett, and Shields 2001). Preschoolers' ability to interpret dangerous objects or situations in their environments is limited by their capacity for causal reasoning. Building understanding of safety issues and safety rules through a participatory, problem-solving curriculum was shown to improve elementary children's injury risk behavior (Morrongiello, Midgett, and Shields 2001). However, Rivara and others (1991) indicate that children do not have the ability to evaluate risk or to make smart risk decisions until they are seven or eight years old. If safety-education curricula assume preschoolers have developed causal reasoning skills, these programs might be either ineffective or confusing to children who have limited understanding of cause-and-effect relationships (Coppens 1985).

In a study that examined the effectiveness of a school pedestrian training program for children in kindergarten through grade four, only modest changes in pedestrian behavior were achieved. The authors suggest that beginning the program in preschool was not feasible because of the developmental abilities of preschool children (Rivara and others 1991). The authors argue that the skills needed to handle traffic safety exceed the abilities of the child at this developmental age. They suggest that pedestrian safety-education for preschool children needs to be set in a larger program of supervision and protection of children by adults.

Nutrition

Children learn about food through the direct experience of eating, by observing the eating behaviors of caregivers and peers (Savage, Fisher, and Birch 2007), and by handling, preparing, and talking about food (Satter 2007).

Nutrition Knowledge

Intervention studies show that preschool children can learn about food groups (Anliker and others 1990; Ellis and Ellis 2007; Hertzler and DeBord 1994), and have some ability to judge relative food values (foods that should be eaten frequently versus foods that should be eaten only sometimes; for example, very sweet or salty foods) (Goldman and others 1991; Gorelick and Clark 1985; Murphy and others 1995). They can judge these relative food values even when those values conflict with their own food preferences (Anliker and others 1990). However, children's food preferences and choices often do not reflect what they know about the nutritional quality of foods (Anliker and others 1990; Klesges and others 1991; Murphy and others 1995; Toporoff and others 1997) Studies also show that when children eat a food as a means to obtain a reward (for example, "Eat your beans and you'll get ice cream for dessert"), children's preference for that food (beans) decreases, and their preference for the reward (the ice cream) actually increases (Birch 1987; Birch and others 1987). Preschool age children also have difficulty understanding the importance of variety in their diets (Murphy and others 1990).

Nutrition Choices

Preschool is an opportunity to encourage the development of sound eating habits and healthy relationships to food (American Dietetic Association 2005). Research conducted over the last 40 years shows that children's food choices are shaped by hereditary tendencies (such as a preference for sweet foods), eating environment (Birch 1987, 1994; Fisher 2005), and by caregiver feeding practices (Hughes and others 2007). Food habits that develop in early childhood persist during the early school years (Williams and Strobino 2008). Preschool programs can influence the establishment of healthy eating preferences and eating behaviors in preschool children (Koblinsky, Guthrie, and Lynch 1992; Nahikian-Nelms 1997).

Children have an internal motivation to eat a variety of foods, including nutritious foods. They learn food preferences based, in part, on repeated exposures to, and social experiences with, food. It is not unusual for children to need 10 to 20 neutral exposures to a new food before they will accept it (Satter 2007; Savage, Fisher, and Birch 2007). However, some children are particularly sensitive to the introduction of new foods (Russell and Worsley 2008).

Obesity is a national health problem (Budd and Hayman 2008). Preschool children are exceeding the recommendations for saturated fat intake. Eighty percent of schoolchildren do not consume the recommended five or more servings of fruits and vegetables per day (Hayman and others 2004). Children with high or low levels of food intake tend to maintain those levels over time (Singer and others 1995). Eating patterns that increase children's risk of future cardiovascular disease are learned early. Preschool programs that involve teachers and parents, as well as children, have been shown to be effective in promoting the adoption of heart-healthy behaviors and reducing risk factors for cardiovascular disease (Hayman and others 2007).

Self-Regulation of Eating

Most infants are born with the ability to self-regulate their calorie intake. When children are allowed to serve themselves and choose what they eat, they learn to pay attention to their internal cues of hunger and satiety (fullness): to recognize when they are full and stop eating (Francis, Hofer, and Birch 2001; Galloway and others 2006; Johnson 2000; Satter 2007; Savage, Fisher, and Birch 2007). Johnson (2000) found that an intervention study helping preschool children to identify and pay attention to internal cues of hunger and satiety improved their ability to self-regulate food intake. Johnson reports, however, that her study does not support the idea that children are capable of making healthy food choices without adult guidance. She argues that adults' responsibility for acting as positive role models may be more important than previously recognized.

Satter's (2007) views about the division of responsibility in feeding have had a significant impact on the early childhood profession. According to Satter, children should be responsible for whether and how much they eat and should be encouraged by caregivers to pay attention to internal cues of hunger and fullness. Adults are responsible for what foods are offered and when and where they are offered. They should also respect children's choices about what they eat, how much they eat, and when they say they are full. The end result is that children learn to regulate how much they eat.

Food insecurity plays a role in the loss of self-regulation and disproportionately affects low-income and minority households. African Americans, Hispanics, and households with children experience food insecurity at almost double the rate of households without children. California children from low-income families are at a greater risk of becoming overweight or obese. One in five California teens in families at or below the federal poverty level (FPL) is overweight or obese compared with less than one in 10 teens at 300 percent above the FPL. This finding is due, in large part, to the high costs of healthy foods (Children Now 2009).

Glossary

caries. Also known as tooth decay. It is a disease that causes destruction of tooth enamel and irritation of the gums surrounding the teeth. It occurs when foods containing carbohydrates (sugars and starches) are frequently left on the teeth. Bacteria that live in the mouth thrive on these foods, converting them into acids. Over a period of time, these acids dissolve tooth enamel, resulting in cavities (holes in the teeth).

cavities. Holes in the teeth.

family-style meals. Meals in which food is served in common dishes from which children serve themselves. Children pass the serving dishes from child to child, taking as much or as little food as they want. Caregivers participate in the meal, modeling good eating habits, taking part in conversations, and assisting children only when the child requests help.

food insecurity. The limited or uncertain availability of nutritionally adequate and safe foods or the uncertain ability to acquire appropriate foods in socially acceptable ways (Anderson 1990). Food insecurity often leads to buying less-nutritious food that is high in calories and fat. Groups with the highest prevalence of household food insecurity are African Americans (22 percent of households), Latinos (18 percent of households), households with children younger than six years (17 percent), and single-mother households (31 percent) (Nord, Andrews, and Carlson 2007).

food-secure. Assured access at all times to enough high-quality food for an active, healthy life and without the need to seek emergency food sources or use other extraordinary coping behaviors to meet basic food needs.

handwashing routine. Use soap to make lather, rub backs and fronts and in between fingers, rinse with running water, dry hands, turn off the faucet with a paper towel, and dispose of the paper towel.

infestation. The presence of a large number of pests (for example, lice or pinworms).

precausal reasoning. Piaget's description of the reasoning of young children, which does not follow the procedures of either deductive or inductive reasoning. According to Piaget, young children believe that people can make things happen; however, children do not have an understanding of the invisible physical and mechanical forces that cause things to happen.

preoperational stage. According to Piagetian theory, it is the period between ages two and six. A child learns to use language, representing things with words and images, but does not yet understand concrete logic. The child cannot mentally manipulate information and is unable to take the point of view of other people or think through the consequences of an action.

scaffolding. A term borrowed from the construction industry that refers to a temporary framework that supports a building during construction. When the building is sturdy enough to stand on its own, the scaffolding is removed. In education, scaffolding involves supporting children's learning of new skills or concepts until children can complete a skill or understand a concept on their own, and the supports are withdrawn. For example, children who are too young to understand that germs spread disease are taught to wash their hands; they do it because a teacher tells them, "This is what we do." When they are older, they wash their hands because they understand that if they do not, they are more likely to get sick. They no longer need the teacher's instruction and direction to know how and when to wash their hands. It is also easier for the child to remember to wash hands because it has become an embodied habit or practice.

scripts. Rules of behavior. Scripts describe a sequence of behaviors associated with a given situation or task (for example, brushing teeth). Scripts are used to develop habits and practices. Following scripts saves time and the mental effort of figuring out an appropriate behavior each time a situation is encountered. Scripts are a way to habituate preschool children to important health practices such as handwashing, physical activity, pedestrian safety, and so on.

toothbrushing routine. The steps are as follows: Place smear of toothpaste (from child's own tube or from a piece of paper or the edge of a paper plate) on brush; with brush at gum line at 45-degree angle, make small circles brushing the outer, inner, and flat surfaces of the upper and lower teeth and tongue for two minutes; rinse; spit.

References and Source Materials

American Academy of Pediatrics; American Public Health Association; and National Resource Center for Health and Safety in Child Care and Early Education. 2002. *Caring for Our Children: National Health and Safety Performance Standards: Guidelines for Out-of-Home Child Care* (Second edition). Elk Grove Village, IL: American Academy of Pediatrics.

American Dietetic Association. 2005. "Position of the American Dietetic Association: Benchmarks for Nutrition Programs in Child Care Settings," *Journal of the American Dietetic Association,* Vol. 105, No. 6, 979–86.

Anderson, S. A. 1990. "Core Indicators of Nutritional Status for Difficult-to-Sample Populations," *Journal of Nutrition,* Vol. 120, No. 11S, 1559–1600.

Anliker, J. A., and others. 1990. "Parental Messages and the Nutrition Awareness of Preschool Children," *Journal of Nutrition Education,* Vol. 22, No. 1, 24–29.

Barker, J. C., and S. B. Horton. 2008. "An Ethnographic Study of Latino Preschool Children's Oral Health in Rural California: Intersections Among Family, Community, Provider and Regulatory Sectors," *BMC Oral Health,* Vol. 8, 8.

Bibace, R., and M. E. Walsh. 1980. "Development of Children's Concepts of Illness," *Pediatrics,* Vol. 66, No. 6, 912–17.

Birch, L. L. 1987. "The Role of Experience in Children's Food Acceptance Patterns," *Journal of the American Dietetic Association,* Vol. 87, Supplement 9, S36–S40.

Birch, L. L. 1994. "How Kids Choose Foods." Paper presented at the International Conference on Gastronomy, Monterey, CA, March 1994.

Birch, L. L., and others. 1987. "What Kind of Exposure Reduces Children's Food Neophobia? Looking vs. Tasting," *Appetite,* Vol. 9, No. 3, 171–78.

Blumenshine, S. L., and others. 2008. "Children's School Performance: Impact of General and Oral Health," *Journal of Public Health Dentistry,* Vol. 68, No. 2, 82–87.

Borse, N., and others. 2008. *CDC Childhood Injury Report: Patterns of Unintentional Injuries Among 0–19 Year Olds in the United States, 2000–2006.* Atlanta, GA: The Centers for Disease Control and Prevention.

Braveman, P.; T. Sadegh-Nobariand; and S. Ergerter. 2008. *Early Childhood Experiences and Health: Laying the Foundation for Health Across a Lifetime: Report from the Robert Wood Johnson Foundation to the Commission to Build a Healthier America.* Princeton, NJ: The Robert Wood Johnson Foundation.

Budd, G. M., and L. L. Hayman. 2008. "Addressing the Childhood Obesity Crisis: A Call to Action," *MCN American Journal of Maternal Child Nursing,* Vol. 33, No. 2, 111–18, quiz 119–20.

California Code of Regulations, Title 22, Division 12, Chapter 1, Article 6 (Cont.) Child Care Centers General Licensing Requirements (101226). 2005. Sacramento: California Department of Social Services. http://www.dss.cahwnet.gov/ord/entres/getinfo/pdf/ccc5.pdf (accessed April 2, 2009).

California Department of Education. 2008. *Nutrition Competencies for California's Children.* http://www.cde.ca.gov/ls/nu/he/ncccindex.asp (accessed May 18, 2009).

Carey, S. 1985. *Conceptual Change in Childhood.* Cambridge, MA: MIT Press.

Children Now. 2009. *California Report Card 2009: Setting the Agenda for Children.* Oakland, CA: Children Now.

Children's Safety Network National Resource Center. N.d. California Fact Sheet. http://www.childrenssafetynetwork.org/publications_resources/PDF/factsheets/CA.pdf (accessed February 20, 2009).

Cook, J. T., and D. A. Frank. 2008. "Food Security, Poverty, and Human Development in the United States," *Annals of the New York Academy of Sciences,* Vol. 1136, 193–209.

Coppens, N. 1985. "Cognitive Development and Locus of Control as Predictors of Preschoolers' Understanding of Safety and Prevention," *Journal of Applied Developmental Psychology,* Vol. 6, No.1, 43–55.

Curnow, M. M., and others. 2002. "A Randomised Controlled Trial of the Efficacy of Supervised Tooth Brushing in High-Caries-Risk Children," *Caries Research,* Vol. 36, No. 4, 294–300.

Dental Health Foundation. 2006. "Mommy, It Hurts to Chew," *The California Smile Survey: An Oral Health Assessment of California's Kindergarten and 3rd Grade Children.* Oakland, CA: The Dental Health Foundation.

Dickens, M. D., and others. 1992. "The Medical Home: Ad Hoc Task Force on Definition of the Medical Home," *Pediatrics,* Vol. 90, No. 5, 774.

Eiser, C. 1989. "Children's Concepts of Illness: Towards an Alternative to the 'Stage' Approach," *Psychology and Health,* Vol. 3, No. 2, 93–101.

Ellis, R. M., and R. C. Ellis. 2007. "Impact of a Traffic Light Nutrition Tool in a Primary School," *Journal of the Royal Society for the Promotion of Health,* Vol. 127, No. 1, 13–21.

Fischer, K. W. 1980. "A Theory of Cognitive Development: The Control and Construction of Hierarchies of Skills," *Psychological Review,* Vol. 87, 477–531.

Fisher, J. O. 2005. "Promoting Healthy Eating: What Research Says That Parents Need to Know." Paper presented at Nutrition Connections, the 2nd National Nutrition Education Conference, Arlington, VA, September 2005.

Flores, G., and S. Tomany-Korman. 2008. "The Language Spoken at Home and Disparities in Medical and Dental Health, Access to Care and Use of Services in U.S. Children," *Pediatrics,* Vol. 121, No. 6, 1703–14.

Francis, L. A.; S. M. Hofer; and L. L. Birch. 2001. "Predictors of Maternal Child-Feeding Style: Maternal and Child Characteristics," *Appetite,* Vol. 37, No. 3, 231–43.

Galloway, A. T., and others. 2006. " 'Finish your soup': Counterproductive Effects of Pressuring Children to Eat on Intake and Affect," *Appetite,* Vol. 46, No. 3, 318-323.

Goldman, S. L., and others. 1991. "Children's Representations of 'Everyday' Aspects of Health and Illness," *Journal of Pediatric Psychology,* Vol. 16, No. 6, 747–66.

Gorelick, M., and E. Clark. 1985. "Effects of a Nutrition Program on Knowledge of Preschool Children," *Journal of Nutrition Education and Behavior,* Vol. 17, No. 3, 88–92.

Gupta, R. S., and others. 2005. "Opportunities for Health Promotion Education in Child Care," *Pediatrics,* Vol. 116, No. 4, 499–505.

Guyer, B., and others. 2008. *Investments to Promote Children's Health: A Systematic Literature Review and Economic Analysis of Interventions in the Preschool Period.* Baltimore, MD: Women's and Children's Health Policy Center, John Hopkins Bloomberg School of Public Health.

Hahn, E. J., and others. 2000. "Kindergarten Children's Knowledge and Perceptions of Alcohol, Tobacco, and Other Drugs," *Journal of School Health,* Vol. 70, No. 2, 51–55.

Hardy, M. S. 2002. "Teaching Firearm Safety to Children: Failure of a

Program," *Journal of Developmental Behaviorial Pediatrics*, Vol. 23, No. 2, 71–76.

Hayman, L. L., and others. 2004. "Cardiovascular Health Promotion in the Schools: A Statement for Health and Education Professionals and Child Health Advocates from the Committee on Atherosclerosis, Hypertension, and Obesity in Youth of the Council on Cardiovascular Disease in the Young, American Heart Association," *Circulation*, Vol. 110, No. 15, 2266–75.

Hayman, L. L., and others. 2007. "Primary Prevention of Cardiovascular Disease in Nursing Practice: Focus on Children and Youth. A Scientific Statement from the American Heart Association Committee on Atherosclerosis, Hypertension, and Obesity in Youth of the Council on Cardiovascular Disease in the Young, Council on Cardiovascular Nursing, Council on Epidemiology and Prevention, and Council on Nutrition, Physical Activity, and Metabolism," *Circulation*, Vol. 116, No. 3, 344–57.

Hendrickson, D.; C. Smith; and N. Eikenberry. 2006. "Fruit and Vegetable Access in Four Low-Income Food Deserts Communities in Minnesota," *Agriculture and Human Values*, Vol. 23, No. 3, 371–83.

Hertzler, A. A., and K. DeBord. 1994. "Preschoolers' Developmentally Appropriate Food and Nutrition Skills," *Journal of Nutrition Education and Behavior*, Vol. 26, 166B.

Hughes, S. O., and others. 2007. "The Impact of Child Care Providers' Feeding on Children's Food Consumption," *Journal of Developmental Behavioral Pediatrics*, Vol. 28, No. 2, 100–07.

Inagaki, K., and G. Hatano. 2004. "Vitalistic Causality in Young Children's Naive Biology," *Trends in Cognitive Sciences*, Vol. 8, No. 8, 356–62.

Johnson, S. L. 2000. "Improving Preschoolers' Self-Regulation of Energy Intake," *Pediatrics*, Vol. 106, No. 6, 1429–35.

Kalish, C. 1996. "Causes and Symptoms in Preschoolers' Conceptions of Illness," *Child Development*, Vol. 67, No. 4, 1647–70.

Kalish, C. 1999. "What Young Children's Understanding of Contamination and Contagion Tells Us About Their Concepts of Illness," in *Children's Understanding of Biology and Health*, 99–130. Edited by M. Siegal and C. C. Peterson. Cambridge: Cambridge University Press.

Kalnins, I., and R. Love. 1982. "Children's Concepts of Health and Illness—and Implications for Health Education: An Overview," *Health Education and Behavior*, Vol. 9, No. 2-3, 8–12.

Klesges, R. C., and others. 1991. "Parental Influence on Food Selection in Young Children and Its Relationships to Childhood Obesity" [published erratum appears in *American Journal of Clinical Nutrition*, December 1991, Vol. 54, No. 6, 4], *American Journal of Clinical Nutrition*, Vol. 53, No. 4, 859–64.

Koblinsky, S. A.; J. F. Guthrie; and L. Lynch. 1992. "Evaluation of a Nutrition Education Program for Head Start Parents," *Journal of Nutrition Education and Behavior*, Vol. 24, No. 1, 4–13.

Koopman, H. M., and others. 2004. "Illness Through the Eyes of the Child: The Development of Children's Understanding of the Causes of Illness," *Patient Education and Counseling*, Vol. 55, No. 3, 363–70.

Kramer, R. A.; L. Allen; and P. J. Gergen. 1995. "Health and Social Characteristics and Children's Cognitive Functioning: Results from a National Cohort," *American Journal of Public Health*, Vol. 85, No. 3, 312–18.

Lees, N. B., and B. J. Tinsley. 1998. "Patterns of Parental Socialization of the Preventive Health Behavior of Young Mexican Origin Children," *Journal of Applied Developmental Psychology*, Vol. 19, No. 4, 503–25.

Loescher, L. J., and others. 1995. "Educating Preschoolers about Sun Safety," *American Journal of Public Health,* Vol. 85, No. 7, 939–43.

MacNeal, R. J., and J. G Dinulos. 2007. "Update on Sun Protection and Tanning in Children," *Current Opinion in Pediatrics,* Vol. 19, No. 4, 425–29.

McPherson M., and others. 1998 "A New Definition of Children with Special Health Care Needs," *Pediatrics,* Vol. 102, No. 1, 137–40.

McWhirter, J. M., and others. 2000. "Evaluating 'Safe in the Sun,' a Curriculum Programme for Primary Schools," *Health Education Research,* Vol. 15, No. 2, 203–17.

Mendelson, K. G., and, M. E. Fallat. 2007. "Pediatric Injuries: Prevention to Resolution," *Surgical Clinic of North America,* Vol. 87, No. 1, 207–28.

Morrongiello, B. A.; C. Midgett; and R. Shields. 2001. "Don't Run with Scissors: Young Children's Knowledge of Home Safety Rules," *Journal of Pediatric Psychology,* Vol. 26, No. 2, 105–15.

Morrongiello, B. A.; J. Miron; and R. Reutz. 1998. "Prevention of Paediatric Acquired Brain Injury: An Interactive, Elementary-School Program," *Canadian Journal of Public Health,* Vol. 89, No. 6, 391–96.

Murphy, A. S., and others. 1995. "Kindergarten Students' Food Preferences Are Not Consistent with Their Knowledge of the Dietetic Guidelines," *Journal of the American Dietician Association,* Vol. 95, No. 2, 219–23.

Murphy, S. P., and others. 1990. "An Evaluation of Food Group Intakes by Mexican-American Children," *Journal of the American Dietician Association,* Vol. 90, No. 3, 388–93.

Nahikian-Nelms, M. 1997. "Influential Factors of Caregiver Behavior at Mealtime: A Study of 24 Child-Care Programs," *Journal of the American Dietetic Association,* Vol. 97, 505–50.

National Association for the Education of Young Children. 2005. *NAEYC Early Childhood Program Standards and Accreditation Criteria: The Mark of Quality in Early Childhood Education.* Washington, DC: NAEYC.

National Association of Child Care Resource and Referral Agencies (NACCRRA). 2008. Child Care in America. Arlington, VA: National Association of Child Care Resource and Referral Agencies. http://www.naccrra.org/policy/docs/ChildCareinAmerica.pdf (accessed February 23, 2009).

Nelson, K., and J. Gruendel. 1986. "Children's Scripts," in *Event Knowledge: Structure and Function in Development.* Edited by K. Nelson. Hillsdale, NJ: Lawrence Erlbaum.

Newacheck, P. W., and others. 2008. "Who Is at Risk for Special Health Care Needs: Findings From the National Survey of Children's Health," *Pediatrics,* Vol. 122, No. 2, 347–59.

Niffenegger, J. P. 1997. "Proper Handwashing Promotes Wellness in Child Care," *Journal of Pediatric Health Care,* Vol. 11, No. 1, 26–31.

Nord, M,; M. Andrews; and S. Carlson. 2007. "Measuring Food Security in the United States: Household Food Security in the United States, 2005," *USDA Economic Research Service, Economic Research Report No. 9.* Washington, DC. http://www.ers.usda.gov/Publications/ERR29/ERR29.pdf (accessed February 23, 2009).

Palfrey, J. S., and others. 2005. "The Brookline Early Education Project: A 25-Year Follow-Up Study of a Family-Centered Early Health and Development Intervention," *Pediatrics,* Vol. 116, No.1, 144–52.

Poche, C.; H. McCubbrey; and T. Munn. 1988. "The Development of Correct Toothbrushing Technique in Preschool Children," *Journal of Applied Behavior Analysis,* Vol. 15, No. 2, 315–20.

Popkin, B. M.; K. Duffey; and P. Gordon-Larsen. 2005. "Environmental Influences on Food Choice, Physical Activity and Energy Balance," *Physiology and Behavior,* Vol. 86, No. 5, 603–13.

Rivara, F. P., and others. 1991. "Prevention of Pedestrian Injuries to Children: Effectiveness of a School Training Program," *Pediatrics,* Vol. 88, No. 4, 770–75.

Rong, W. S., and others. 2003. "Effectiveness of an Oral Health Education and Caries Prevention Program in Kindergartens in China," *Community Dentistry and Oral Epidemiology,* Vol. 31, No. 6, 412–16.

Rosen, L., and others. 2006. "Can a Handwashing Intervention Make a Difference? Results from a Randomized Controlled Trial in Jerusalem Preschools," *Preventive Medicine,* Vol. 42, No. 1, 27–32.

Rozin, P., and A. Fallon. 1980. "The Psychological Categorization of Foods and Non-Foods: A Preliminary Taxonomy of Food Rejections," *Appetite,* Vol. 1, 193–201.

Rozin, P., and T. A. Vollmecke. 1986. "Food Likes and Dislikes," *Annual Review of Nutrition,* Vol. 6, 433–56.

Russell, C. G., and A. Worsley. 2008. "A Population-Based Study of Preschoolers' Food Neophobia and Its Associations with Food Preferences," *Journal of Nutrition Education and Behavior,* Vol. 40, No. 1, 11–19.

Saha, S.; A. Fernandez; and E. Perez-Stable. 2007. "Reducing Language Barriers and Racial/Ethnic Disparities in Health Care: An Investment in Our Future," *Journal of General Internal Medicine,* Vol. 22, Supplement 2, 371–72.

Satter, E. 2007. "Eating Competence: Nutrition Education with the Satter Eating Competence Model," *Journal of Nutrition Education and Behavior,* Vol. 39, Supplement 5, S189–94.

Savage, J. S., J. O. Fisher, and L. L. Birch. 2007. "Parental Influence on Eating Behavior: Conception to Adolescence," *Journal of Law, Medicine and Ethics,* Vol. 35, No. 1, 22–34.

Siegal, M. 1988. "Children's Knowledge of Contagion and Contamination as Causes of Illness," *Child Development,* Vol. 59, No. 5, 1353–59.

Singer, M. R., and others. 1995. "The Tracking of Nutrient Intake in Young Children: The Framingham Children's Study," *American Journal of Public Health,* Vol. 85, No. 12, 1673–77.

Slaughter, V.; R. Jaakkola; and S. Carey. 1999. "Constructing a Coherent Theory: Children's Biological Understanding of Life and Death," in *Children's Understanding of Biology and Health,* 71–96. Edited by M. Siegal and C. Peterson. Cambridge: Cambridge University Press.

Spernak, S. M., and others. 2006. "Child Health and Academic Achievement Among Former Head Start Children," *Children and Youth Services Review,* Vol. 28, No. 10, 1251–61.

Springer, K., and J. Ruckel. 1992. "Early Beliefs About the Cause of Illness: Evidence Against Immanent Justice," *Cognitive Development,* Vol. 7, No. 4, 429–43.

Stevens, G. D., and others. 2009. "National Disparities in the Quality of a Medical Home for Children," *Maternal and Child Health Journal.* http://www.springerlink.com/content/x8nr8704uw5u645j (accessed February 20, 2009).

Sullivan, S. A., and L. L. Birch. 1990. "Pass the Sugar, Pass the Salt: Experience Dictates Preference," *Developmental Psychology,* Vol. 26, No. 4, 546–51.

Taveras, E. M., and others. 2006. "Planning for Health Promotion in Low-Income Preschool Child Care Settings: Focus Groups of Parents and Child Care Providers," *Ambulatory Pediatrics,* Vol. 6, No. 6, 342–46.

Thies, K. 1999. "Identifying the Educational Implications of Chronic Illness in School Children," *The Journal of School Health,* Vol. 69, 392–7.

Tinsley, B. J. 2003. *How Children Learn to Be Healthy.* Cambridge, UK: Cambridge University Press.

Toporoff, E. G., and others. 1997. "Do Children Eat What They Say? Validity of Intended Food Choices Among Native American School Children," *Obesity Research,* Vol. 5, No. 2, 87–92.

U.S. Department of Health and Human Services (HHS). 2000a. *Healthy People 2010: Understanding and Improving Health.* http://minority-health.pitt.edu/archive/00000640/ (accessed February 27, 2008).

U.S. Department of Health and Human Services (HHS). 2000b. *Oral Health in America: A Report of the Surgeon General.* Rockville, MD: HHS, National Institutes of Health, National Institute of Dental and Craniofacial Research.

Van Dyck, P. C., and others. 2004. "Prevalence and Characteristics of Children with Special Health Care Needs," *Archives of Pediatric and Adolescent Medicine,* Vol. 158, No. 9, 884–90.

Vygotsky, L. S. 1978. *Mind and Society: The Development of Higher Psychological Processes.* Cambridge, MA: Harvard University Press.

Wennhall, I., and others. 2005. "Caries-Preventive Effect of an Oral Health Program for Preschool Children in a Low Socio-Economic, Multicultural Area in Sweden: Results After One Year," *Acta Odontologica Scandinavica,* Vol. 63, No. 3, 163–67.

Wilkinson, S. R. 1988. *The Child's World of Illness: The Development of Health and Illness Behavior.* Cambridge, UK: Cambridge University Press.

Williams, C. L., and others. 1998. "Healthy Start: A Comprehensive Health Education Program for Preschool Children," *Preventive Medicine,* Vol. 27, No. 2, 216–23.

Williams, C. L., and B. A. Strobino. 2008. "Childhood Diet, Overweight, and CVD Risk Factors: The Healthy Start Project," *Preventive Cardiology,* Vol. 11, No. 1, 11–20.

Williams, J. M., and L. M. Binnie. 2002. "Children's Concept of Illness: An Intervention to Improve Knowledge," *British Journal of Health Psychology,* Vol. 7, No. 2, 129–48.

Wolfe, B. L. 1985. "The Influence of Health on School Outcomes. A Multivariate Approach," *Medical Care,* Vol. 23, No. 10, 1127–38.

APPENDIX

The Foundations

Visual and Performing Arts

Visual Art

1.0 Notice, Respond, and Engage

At around 48 months of age	*At around 60 months of age*
1.1 Notice and communicate about objects or forms that appear in art.	1.1 Communicate about elements appearing in art (such as line, texture, or perspective), and describe how objects are positioned in the artwork.
1.2 Create marks with crayons, paints, and chalk and then identify them; mold and build with dough and clay and then identify them.	1.2 Begin to plan art and show increasing care and persistence in completing it.
1.3 Enjoy and engage with displays of visual art, inside or outside the classroom. Begin to express preferences for some art activities or materials.	1.3 Enjoy and engage with displays of visual art. May expand critical assessment of visual art to include preferences for types of artwork or art activities.
1.4 Choose own art for display in the classroom or for inclusion in a portfolio or book and briefly explain choice.	1.4 Choose own art for display in the classroom or for inclusion in a portfolio or book and explain her or his ideas in some detail.

2.0 Develop Skills in Visual Art

2.1 Make straight and curved marks and lines; begin to draw rough circle shapes.	2.1 Draw single circle and add lines to create representations of people and things.
2.2 Begin to create paintings or drawings that suggest people, animals, and objects.	2.2 Begin to create representative paintings or drawings that approximate or depict people, animals, and objects.

2.0 Develop Skills in Visual Art *(Continued)*

At around 48 months of age	*At around 60 months of age*
2.3 Make somewhat regular-shaped balls and coils out of dough or clay.	2.3 Make more representational forms out of dough or clay, using tools (for example, a rolling pin or a garlic press).
2.4 Begin to use paper and other materials to assemble simple collages.	2.4 Use paper and other materials to make two- and three-dimensional assembled works.
2.5 Begin to recognize and name materials and tools used for visual arts.	2.5 Recognize and name materials and tools used for visual arts.
2.6 Demonstrate some motor control when working with visual arts tools.	2.6 Demonstrate increasing coordination and motor control when working with visual arts tools.

3.0 Create, Invent, and Express Through Visual Art

3.1 Create art and sometimes name the work.	3.1 Intentionally create content in a work of art.
3.2 Begin to draw figures or objects.	3.2 Draw more detailed figures or objects with more control of line and shape.
3.3 Begin to use intensity of marks and color to express a feeling or mood.	3.3 Use intensity of marks and color more frequently to express a feeling or mood.

Music

1.0 Notice, Respond, and Engage

At around 48 months of age	At around 60 months of age
1.1 Sustain attention and begin to reflect verbally about music; demonstrate familiarity with words that describe music.	1.1 Verbally reflect on music and describe music by using an expanded vocabulary.
1.2 Recognize simple repeating melody and rhythm patterns.	1.2 Demonstrate more complex repeating melody and rhythm patterns.
1.3 Identify the sources of a limited variety of musical sounds.	1.3 Identify the sources of a wider variety of music and music-like sounds.
1.4 Use body movement freely to respond loosely to beat—loud versus quiet (dynamics)—and tempo.	1.4 Use body movement freely and more accurately to respond to beat, dynamics, and tempo of music.

2.0 Develops Skills in Music

2.1 Begin to discriminate between different voices and certain instrumental and environmental sounds. Follow words in a song.	2.1 Become more able to discriminate between different voices and various instrumental and environmental sounds. Follow words in a song.
2.2 Explore vocally; sing repetitive patterns and parts of songs alone and with others.	2.2 Extend vocal exploration; sing repetitive patterns and entire songs alone and with others in wider ranges of pitch.

3.0 Create, Invent, and Express Through Music

3.1 Explore vocal and instrumental skills and use instruments to produce simple rhythms and tones.	3.1 Continue to apply vocal and instrumental skills and use instruments to produce more complex rhythms, tones, melodies, and songs.
3.2 Move or use body to demonstrate beat and tempo, often spontaneously.	3.2 Move or use body to demonstrate beat, tempo, and style of music, often intentionally.
3.3 Improvise vocally and instrumentally.	3.3 Explore, improvise, and create brief melodies with voice or instrument.

Drama

1.0 Notice, Respond, and Engage

At around 48 months of age	At around 60 months of age
1.1 Demonstrate an understanding of simple drama vocabulary.	1.1 Demonstrate a broader understanding of drama vocabulary.
1.2 Identify preferences and interests related to participating in drama.	1.2 Explain preferences and interests related to participating in drama.
1.3 Demonstrate knowledge of simple plot of a participatory drama.	1.3 Demonstrate knowledge of extended plot and conflict of a participatory drama.

2.0 Develop Skills to Create, Invent, and Express Through Drama

2.1 Demonstrate basic role-play skills with imagination and creativity.	2.1 Demonstrate extended role-play skills with increased imagination and creativity.
2.2 Add props and costumes to enhance dramatization of familiar stories and fantasy play with peers.	2.2 Create and use an increasing variety of props, costumes and scenery to enhance dramatization of familiar stories and fantasy play with peers.

Dance

1.0 Notice, Respond, and Engage

1.1 Engage in dance movements.	1.1 Further engage and participate in dance movements.
1.2 Begin to understand and use vocabulary related to dance.	1.2 Connect dance terminology with demonstrated steps.
1.3 Respond to instruction of one skill at a time during movement, such as a jump or fall.	1.3 Respond to instruction of more than one skill at a time in movement, such as turning, leaping, and turning again. Often initiate a sequence of skills.
1.4 Explore and use different steps and movements to create or form a dance.	1.4 Use understanding of different steps and movements to create or form a dance.

2.0 Develop Skills in Dance

At around 48 months of age	At around 60 months of age
2.1 Begin to be aware of own body in space.	2.1 Continue to develop awareness of body in space.
2.2 Begin to be aware of other people in dance or when moving in space.	2.2 Show advanced awareness and coordination of movement with other people in dance or when moving in space.
2.3 Begin to respond to tempo and timing through movement.	2.3 Demonstrate some advanced skills in responding to tempo and timing through movement.

3.0 Create, Invent, and Express Through Dance

3.1 Begin to act out and dramatize through music and movement patterns.	3.1 Extend understanding and skills for acting out and dramatizing through music and movement patterns.
3.2 Invent dance movements.	3.2 Invent and recreate dance movements.
3.3 Improvise simple dances that have a beginning and an end.	3.3 Improvise more complex dances that have a beginning, middle, and an end.
3.4 Communicate feelings spontaneously through dance and begin to express simple feelings intentionally through dance when prompted by adults.	3.4 Communicate and express feelings intentionally through dance.

Physical Development

Fundamental Movement Skills

1.0 Balance

At around 48 months of age	At around 60 months of age
1.1 Maintain balance while holding still; sometimes may need assistance.	1.1 Show increasing balance and control when holding still.
1.2 Maintain balance while in motion when moving from one position to another or when changing directions, though balance may not be completely stable.	1.2 Show increasing balance control while moving in different directions and when transitioning from one movement or position to another.

2.0 Locomotor Skills

At around 48 months of age	At around 60 months of age
2.1 Walk with balance, not always stable, oppositional arm movements still developing, and relatively wide base of support (space between feet).	2.1 Walk with balance, oppositional arm movements, and relatively narrow base of support (space between feet).
2.2 Run with short stride length and feet off the ground for a short period of time. May show inconsistent opposition of arms and legs.	2.2 Run with a longer stride length and each foot off the ground for a greater length of time. Opposition of arms and legs is more consistent.
2.3 Jump for height (up or down) and for distance with beginning competence.	2.3 Jump for height (up or down) and for distance with increasing competence. Uses arm swing to aid forward jump.
2.4 Begin to demonstrate a variety of locomotor skills, such as galloping, sliding, hopping, and leaping.	2.4 Demonstrate increasing ability and body coordination in a variety of locomotor skills, such as galloping, sliding, hopping, and leaping.

3.0 Manipulative Skills

At around 48 months of age	At around 60 months of age
3.1 Begin to show gross motor manipulative skills by using arms, hands, and feet, such as rolling a ball underhand, tossing underhand, bouncing, catching, striking, throwing overhand, and kicking.	3.1 Show gross motor manipulative skills by using arms, hands, and feet with increased coordination, such as rolling a ball underhand, tossing underhand, bouncing, catching, striking, throwing overhand, and kicking.
3.2 Begin to show fine motor manipulative skills using hands and arms such as in-hand manipulation, writing, cutting, and dressing.	3.2 Show increasing fine motor manipulative skills using hands and arms such as in-hand manipulation, writing, cutting, and dressing.

Perceptual–Motor Skills and Movement Concepts

1.0 Body Awareness

At around 48 months of age	At around 60 months of age
1.1 Demonstrate knowledge of the names of body parts.	1.1 Demonstrate knowledge of an increasing number of body parts.

2.0 Spatial Awareness

2.1 Use own body as reference point when locating or relating to other people or objects in space.	2.1 Use own body, general space, and other people's space when locating or relating to other people or objects in space.

3.0 Directional Awareness

3.1 Distinguish movements that are up and down and to the side of the body (for example, understands "use that side, now the other side").	3.1 Begin to understand and distinguish between the sides of the body.
3.2 Move forward and backward or up and down easily.	3.2 Can change directions quickly and accurately.

3.0 Directional Awareness *(Continued)*

At around 48 months of age	At around 60 months of age
3.3 Can place an object on top of or under something with some accuracy.	3.3 Can place an object or own body in front of, to the side, or behind something else with greater accuracy.
3.4 Use any two body parts together.	3.4 Demonstrate more precision and efficiency during two-handed fine motor activities.

Active Physical Play

1.0 Active Participation

At around 48 months of age	At around 60 months of age
1.1 Initiate or engage in simple physical activities for a short to moderate period of time.	1.1 Initiate more complex physical activities for a sustained period of time.

2.0 Cardiovascular Endurance

2.1 Engage in frequent bursts of active play that involves the heart, the lungs, and the vascular system.	2.1 Engage in sustained active play of increasing intensity that involves the heart, the lungs, and the vascular system.

3.0 Muscular Strength, Muscular Endurance, and Flexibility

3.1 Engage in active play activities that enhance leg and arm strength, muscular endurance, and flexibility.	3.1 Engage in increasing amounts of active play activities that enhance leg and arm strength, muscular endurance, and flexibility.

Health

Health Habits

1.0 Basic Hygiene

At around 48 months of age	At around 60 months of age
1.1 Demonstrate knowledge of some steps in the handwashing routine.	1.1 Demonstrate knowledge of more steps in the handwashing routine.
1.2 Practice health habits that prevent infectious diseases and infestations (such as lice) when appropriate, with adult support, instruction, and modeling.	1.2 Begin to independently practice health habits that prevent infectious disease and infestations (such as lice) when appropriate, with less adult support, instruction, and modeling.

2.0 Oral Health

2.1 Demonstrate knowledge of some steps of the routine for brushing teeth, with adult supervision and instruction.	2.1 Demonstrate knowledge of more steps of the routine for brushing and when toothbrushing should be done, with less adult supervision.

3.0 Knowledge of Wellness

3.1 Identify a few internal body parts (most commonly the bones, brain, and heart) but may not understand their basic function.	3.1 Identify several different internal body parts and demonstrate a basic, limited knowledge of some functions.
3.2 Begin to understand that health-care providers try to keep people well and help them when they are not well.	3.2 Demonstrate greater understanding that health-care providers try to keep people well and help them when they are not well.
3.3 Communicate to an adult about not feeling well, feeling uncomfortable, or about a special health need, with varying specificity and reliability.	3.3 Communicate to an adult about not feeling well, feeling uncomfortable, or about a special health need, with more specificity and reliability.

4.0 Sun Safety

4.1 Begin to practice sun-safe actions, with adult support and guidance.	4.1 Practice sun-safe actions with decreasing adult support and guidance.

Safety

1.0 Injury Prevention

At around 48 months of age	*At around 60 months of age*
1.1 Follow safety rules with adult support and prompting.	1.1 Follow safety rules more independently though may still need adult support and prompting.
1.2 Begin to show ability to follow emergency routines after instruction and practice (for example, a fire drill or earthquake drill).	1.2 Demonstrate increased ability to follow emergency routines after instruction and practice.
1.3 Show beginning ability to follow transportation and pedestrian safety rules with adult instruction and supervision.	1.3 Show increased ability to follow transportation and pedestrian safety rules with adult support and supervision.

Nutrition

1.0 Nutrition Knowledge

At around 48 months of age	*At around 60 months of age*
1.1 Identify different kinds of foods.	1.1 Identify a larger variety of foods and may know some of the related food groups.

2.0 Nutrition Choices

2.1 Demonstrate a beginning understanding that eating a variety of food helps the body grow and be healthy, and choose from a variety of foods at mealtimes.	2.1 Demonstrate greater understanding that eating a variety of food helps the body grow and be healthy, and choose from a greater variety of foods at mealtimes.
2.2 Indicate food preferences that reflect familial and cultural practices.	2.2 Indicate food preferences based on familial and cultural practices and on some knowledge of healthy choices.

3.0 Self-Regulation of Eating

3.1 Indicate awareness of own hunger and fullness.	3.1 Indicate greater awareness of own hunger and fullness.